Shares Made Simple

Rodney Hobson

HARRIMAN HOUSE LTD

3A Penns Road
Petersfield
Hampshire
GU32 2EW
GREAT BRITAIN

Tel: +44 (0)1730 233870
Fax: +44 (0)1730 233880
Email: enquiries@harriman-house.com
Website: www.harriman-house.com

First published in Great Britain in 2007
Copyright © Harriman House Ltd

The right of Rodney Hobson to be identified as Author has been asserted
in accordance with the Copyright, Design and Patents Act 1988.

ISBN: 1-905641-45-1
ISBN 13: 978-1905641-45-1

British Library Cataloguing in Publication Data
A CIP catalogue record for this book can be obtained from the British Library.

Photo of Rodney Hobson by Jamil Shehadeh

Printed and bound by the CPI Group 'Antony Rowe, Chippenham'

Index compiled by INDEXING SPECIALISTS (UK) Ltd

Acknowledgments

Marie Hobson, Giles Carey and Naomi Hartley for reading the manuscript and suggesting improvements, Aida Siu for charts and tables, Kevin Sloane of the Association of Private Client Investment Managers and Stockbrokers, and Paul Lucas of Ipreo for permission to use material from the hemscott.com website.

About the author

Rodney Hobson is an experienced financial journalist who has held senior editorial positions with publications in the UK and Asia and is currently Editor of Ipreo, an international financial services group. Among posts he has held are News Editor for the Business section of *The Times*, Business Editor of the *Singapore Monitor*, Deputy Business Editor of the *Far Eastern Economic Review*, Head of News at Citywire and Editor of *Shares* magazine.

He has also contributed to the *Daily Mail*, the *Independent* and *Business Franchise Magazine*.

He is registered as a Representative with the *Financial Services Authority*.

Rodney is married with one daughter.

To Judy

Contents

Section D – Investing

Section E – Takeovers

Appendix

Preface

Who this book is for

This book has been written for those who are new to stock market investment or who want to broaden and deepen their knowledge of how the stock market works.

Anyone wishing to making their own investment decisions, rather than hand their assets over to a fund manager or see them stagnate in bank and building society accounts, will benefit from this carefully crafted step by step guide.

Even people with little spare cash but who want to be informed of the financial world we live in can gain a greater understanding of how the City of London and other business centres operate.

The book is also an invaluable tool for anyone who professionally needs to know about the stock market, from potential wheeler-dealers to advisers, such as auditors and PR, to back office staff and students on business or media courses.

Structure of the book

The book is organised to take readers logically through the various stages of understanding stock market investment, with each new concept explained in simple terms as it arises.

It begins by outlining what shares are, why they exist and why people buy them, followed by a look at the London Stock Exchange and what it is there for.

We discuss how to make sensible decisions on which companies to invest in, sifting the mine of information that is published through the stock exchange, and learn how to pick out the key points in company results, including the warning signs.

With the basics explained, it is time to look at how to buy and sell shares, where to get advice and how to remain well informed.

Finally, we look at takeovers and mergers, the most exciting aspect of stock market investing and the area that offers most scope for making money to investors who, like those who have read this book, understand what is going on.

Supporting website

The accompanying website for the book can be found at:
www.harriman-house.com/sharesmadesimple

Introduction

'My shares have dropped to a fifth of their value', wailed a bewildered shareholder as I picked up his call to the City desk of a national newspaper.

'That's right', I assured him. 'They have been split into five. It was all explained in the document that the company sent out. Had he not read it?'

I could have guessed the answer. No, he had thrown it into the bin because he did not understand it. He did the same with all the documents he received.

A friend with shares in Abbey National received Banco Santander shares in their place when Santander took over Abbey. She told me that she was going to sell her Santander shares because 'I do not want a Spanish bank earning interest on my money'.

Wrong. She was astonished when I explained that she was the one gaining financially, not the bank. And if she felt so strongly about it, why had she ended up with Santander shares when she could so easily have avoided this situation?

Millions of new, unsophisticated investors have been lured into joining the great share owning democracy, first by the privatisation issues and then by the conversion of building societies into banks. They hope for their share of the elusive gold that paves the City of London, the nation's financial heart.

Yet they have only the vaguest notion of what shares are, what they are for or what to do with them.

This long overdue book sets out to put that right. It explains:

- What the stock market is and how it works.

- Why share prices go up and down.

- Why some companies look cheap while others appear to be expensive.

- How to make money and avoid heavy losses.

- The traps that snare the unwary.

By reading this book, you will find that the finance pages of your daily newspaper become a mine of information instead of a daunting mist of incomprehensible murkiness.

You can, if you wish, turn straight to Section D and take a direct leap into the exciting and lucrative world of stock market investing. Or you can use the index to treat this book as a reference work.

However, I would urge all new investors and those with little experience to be patient. Learn to walk before you can run. Start at the beginning and be led logically, step by step, through an easy-to-follow guide to those gold-paved streets. All the baffling issues are dealt with clearly and simply.

I cannot pick your shares for you but I can tell you what to look for and how to look for it. Above all, I will endeavour to provide a level playing field in a world still dominated by professional players as you seek your share of the nation's wealth.

Rodney Hobson
August 2007

SHARES A

1.

What Are Shares?

If you are going to invest through the stock market, we had better start with what it is that you are actually buying.

You will be buying what are known as *ordinary shares*. You, together with all the other investors who have bought shares in a particular company, will become the owners of that company. You have a right to a say in the decision making and you share the profits through the payment of dividends.

These shares are often referred to as *equities*. They represent ownership of the company, just as you have equity in your house: the percentage of your house that you own when the building society's loan is deducted.

The names of the shareholders and the number of shares held will be kept on a share register. Each time a batch of shares changes hands, the new shareholder will be recorded on the register.

There is a difference between running a company and owning it

The day-to-day running of the company will be carried out by a board of directors who may act as if they own the company but they do not. It is you, and the other shareholders, who are the owners. The directors do have the right to own shares. Indeed it is normal for them to buy shares as a show of faith in the company they are running. They have exactly the same rights as shareholders as you do.

Shareholders have the right to attend an annual meeting where they can question the executives who run the company, to receive accounts at least twice a year and to vote for who will be the directors and who will be the auditors. They can approve or veto any proposed major acquisition of another company or the proposed sale of a major part of the existing business.

The number of votes you have and the size of your share of the profits depend on how many shares you own. If you have 1,000 shares in Marks & Spencer and someone else has 10,000 shares then they have 10 times as many votes as you do and they will receive 10 times as much in dividends. Every share carries one equal vote.

Stocks or shares?

In the United Kingdom the two terms stocks and shares have become virtually synonymous but the terms *shares* and *shareholders* are normally used, so these are the terms that will be used in this book.

The Americans tend to refer to stocks but they are talking about the same thing as our shares.

Each share has a *nominal value*. This was the value of each share when the company was originally formed.

If you have a penny black stamp in your possession, it was originally issued back in 1840 for 1p. That is its face value, not its value today. It can be sold for whatever a stamp collector is prepared to pay for it. Similarly you should not expect to pay the nominal face value of a share. You have to pay whatever price the share commands on the stock market.

Where do shares come from?

In the first instance, shares are issued by the company when it is set up. Investors put money in to get the company going. Premises have to be bought or rented, machinery may be needed, staff have to be paid, materials bought... all this before any money comes in from customers. In return, the investors are allocated a stake in the company.

Money, or *capital* as it is referred to, is one of the many inputs that a company needs. Capital can come through the founders putting their hands in their pockets, from taking out bank loans or from selling shares.

The issuing of new shares by the company is known as the *primary market* because it is the first time that the shares have been allocated to investors. When these shares are subsequently bought and sold on the stock market, that is the *secondary market*.

Think of it this way. When a builder puts up a house and sells it for the first time, this is the primary market. When the house is sold on to new owners, that is the secondary market. It is exactly the same with shares.

We shall discuss the primary and secondary markets in chapter two.

Authorised and issued capital

How many shares a company issues is decided by the company itself. There is no fixed number of shares. The number of shares will depend basically on how much capital the company has needed to raise, not only when it was first set up but also at any time subsequently.

All companies have an *authorised share capital*. This sets the maximum number of shares that can be issued. The figure will initially have been set by the original owners of the company and can only be changed by a majority of existing shareholders. That includes you for any company that you have bought shares in.

Not all the authorised capital will be issued. For example, you don't have to drive at 30 mph in a built-up area; that is simply the maximum you are allowed to travel at and you may go more slowly if you like. Similarly authorised capital is a maximum limit. Companies will leave a little leeway in case more capital needs to be raised later.

The shares that have actually been sold by the company to shareholders are the *issued share capital*.

Let us say that a company has 10 million authorised shares with a nominal value of 50p each. Its authorised share capital is £5 million. If it actually issues 8 million shares, its issued share capital is £4 million.

Do not expect such conveniently round numbers. The authorised capital is likely to be a round figure but the issued capital will depend on how much money the company has wanted to raise over the years.

5

For example, insurance company Friends Provident in its 2006 annual report had authorised capital of 2,500 million shares but an issued capital of 2,139,144,969 shares.

Note: that in this book we shall use the now widely accepted usage of 1 billion as being 1,000 million.

Part paid shares

When you buy shares you will almost invariably have to pay up the full amount due immediately but on very rare occasions you may pay for the shares in instalments.

Investors who bought shares in the *privatisation* issues, when the government was selling off state enterprises, may recall that in some cases payments to the government were made in instalments; the idea being that more ordinary investors would be tempted to join the great share owning democracy if they could pay in manageable bits, just like buying a washing machine in monthly instalments.

This is a very messy and expensive arrangement, since some shareholders inevitably forget by the time the third payment is due or they simply do not have the cash. Either way they have to be chased up, which is why part payments rarely happen.

A and B shares

We have assumed so far that you will be buying ordinary shares and that these will rank equally with each other. Each ordinary share has one equal stake in the company and one equal vote.

There is one exception to this, and that is where there are two classes of ordinary shares known as *A shares* and *B shares*.

In the past, some family-owned companies tried to get the best of both worlds, raising cash by selling shares but retaining family ownership by the rather sneaky method of having two classes of shares. A shares, with one vote each, were sold to the general public and B shares, with 10 votes each, were issued to the family. This cunning plot was particularly popular among breweries. It was also used by the Savoy Hotel to keep out that working class bounder Charles Forte.

Thankfully this subterfuge is now regarded as unethical and has all but disappeared. Perhaps the best known name still with two classes of shares is newspaper publisher Daily Mail & General Trust. Its A shares, the ones most widely traded on the stock market, have no votes although there are nearly 400 million of them, while the 20 million ordinary shares control the company. Technically you can also buy the ordinary shares on the stock market but don't bother looking for them; they are rarely traded and just three shareholders held 88.8% of them in mid-2007.

During privatisations you may have come across the Government's *golden share*, which was the ultimate B share. The Government hung on to one share in each privatised company, which could be used to outvote all the other shares put together. This golden share was retained in case the Government felt it needed to intervene in the national interest. Golden shares were used in the UK as a veto only twice and the European Court of Justice has ruled that they are against European law unless national interest is clearly at risk.

Preference shares

There is one other class of shares apart from ordinary shares and they are called *preference shares*. These are in fact more like loans than shares. Preference shareholders do not have voting rights except on issues that specifically affect them. They receive a set rate of interest, usually twice a year, just as you would receive a rate of interest on a savings account in a bank or building society.

It is possible to buy and sell preference shares on the London Stock Exchange in the same way that you buy and sell ordinary shares, although not all companies issue preference shares. Banking group HBOS had three separate sets of preference shares, all paying different rates of interest, traded on the stock market in mid-2007.

Dividends on preference shares must be paid before dividends on ordinary shares and if the company goes bust any cash left over when the creditors have been paid off goes to the preference shareholders first. That's why they are called preference shares.

However, we naturally hope that our investments have gone into prosperous enterprises. While the poor preference shareholders are stuck with a fixed rate of interest, we, the ordinary shareholders, see our dividends rising along with the profits of the company.

As we shall see throughout this book, investors who take the greatest risk expect to receive the greatest reward, and this does tend to happen although there are no guarantees.

Convertibles

Companies raise money by taking out loans, usually by borrowing from the bank through overdrafts or *term loans*, which are loans for a set number of years. They may also borrow from the general public by issuing *loan stock*, also referred to as *bonds*, in much the same way that shares are issued except that holders of loan stock do not own the company.

Some loans can be converted into ordinary shares. These loans are known as *convertibles*.

The terms on which they can be converted, and the dates at which conversion is allowed, will have been set out when the loans were issued. If the loans are at any time converted into ordinary shares, these shares will carry exactly the same rights as those of existing ordinary shares.

Preference shares may be convertible into ordinary shares and will thus be *convertible preference shares*.

2.

How Shares Are Created

The primary market is the creation and sale of new shares. Most of the time you will be buying second-hand shares but we will look first at the different ways in which new shares may be issued to the public.

By the 'public' we do not just mean small investors like yourself or wealthy individuals. Shares are also held by large institutions such as pension funds. We shall refer to these as *institutional investors*.

Initial public offerings

When a company decides that it wants to raise money by issuing shares to the public for the first time it will make what is called an *initial public offering* (more usually referred to by the initials *IPO*).

This is also referred as *coming to market* or a *flotation*.

The shares may be new ones created by the company, in which case any money you spend in buying them will go to the company to be used in expanding the business.

Alternatively, the existing owners may be looking to cash in on their success and are offering some of their shares for sale. In that case, the cash goes to them. The owners may be the people who set up and built the company from scratch and they now want to enjoy the fruits of their labour. It could be a family firm with no-one in the next generation wanting to inherit the business.

Quite often an IPO is a mixture of new shares sold on behalf of the company and a batch of shares from the existing owners.

A *prospectus* giving all relevant details is issued before an IPO takes place. It will state how many shares are being issued, who the directors are and their history and whether there are any skeletons in the cupboard such as outstanding law suits.

Any investor seeking to buy shares in an IPO can contact the company and request a prospectus, although IPO shares are often issued only to institutional and large investors because it is cheaper and simpler than seeking out a large number of small investors.

It is possible in an IPO that the existing owners intend to retain a certain number of shares. The prospectus will spell this out. It will also indicate if the owners have given an undertaking not to sell any or all of their remaining stakes for a specific period of time. This will alert you to the possible danger that a large slab of shares could be dumped onto the market at some future date, depressing the share price.

Rights issue

When a company's shares are already traded on the stock market but it wants to raise more money, it may ask its current shareholders to stump up cash in return for extra shares. This is called a *rights issue* because the shareholders have the right to buy more shares if they want to.

It is only fair that existing shareholders are given the opportunity to buy because, as we shall see, rights issue shares are normally issued at a special low price.

Any rights issue proposed by the directors must by approved by a vote of ordinary shareholders at a special meeting. The right to buy shares will be conferred on shareholders who are on the share register on a specific date.

Under a rights issue the existing shareholders have the right to buy a set number of shares at a set price. Say the rights issue is 1-for-3 at 100p. That means you can buy from the company one new share for every three you already hold and you will pay 100p for each new share that you receive.

The cash goes to the company, usually for a specific purpose such as to make an acquisition or to reduce bank borrowings, but sometimes it is to provide cash in hand for day-to-day running costs or for future needs.

Be sure to read any documents the company sends you regarding a rights issue because in extreme cases the cash may be needed to stop the company going bankrupt.

The discount

The good news about a rights issue is that the price of the new shares is usually set below the stock market price. After all, if you wanted more shares you could buy them on the stock market, so why on earth would you be tempted to pay the same price or more in a rights issue?

The difference between the rights issue price and the stock market price is called the *discount* (assuming that, as normal, the rights price is lower). If it is higher, then the rights issue is at a *premium* to the stock market price.

Case study: Low & Bonar

Low & Bonar, a maker of specialist materials, made a rights issue in July 2006 to help to fund the £71.7m acquisition of Colbond, a producer of synthetic textiles and flooring.

Shareholders were asked to buy one new share for every two they already held. To persuade them to increase their holdings by a hefty 50%, Low offered the new shares at 85p each, which was 35.5% less than the then stock market price of 131.75p.

Since such a large imposition was likely to be declined by many shareholders despite the deep discount to the stock market price, Low arranged for two stockbrokers, Hoare Govett and Numis, to *underwrite* the issue jointly.

The rights issue raised £43.3m but costs, including the underwriting fee, reduced the figure to £41.2m.

Tempted by the discount, shareholders took up 86.2% of the 51m shares on offer. The brokers managed to place the shares with institutional investors at 117p each. Low & Bonar kept 85p and, after deducting the cost of placing the shares, handed about 30p a share to those shareholders who failed to take up their rights.

The size of the discount is decided by the company and it depends on several factors. The more shares on offer, the larger the discount is likely to be. A large discount is referred to as a *deep* discount.

If you are being asked to buy one new share for every one you already own, then you are being asked to double your stake, in which case you will need a strong incentive in the shape of a deep discount to persuade you to empty your pockets. On the other hand, if one new share is available for every 20 you already own, you may think the extra investment is a drop in the ocean and you will be asked to pay a figure close to the stock market price.

The size of the discount will also depend on how desperate the company is for the cash. If it is, in fact, a life saver because the company is in danger of going under than it will have to offer a very deep discount indeed to persuade the unfortunate shareholders to throw good money after bad.

There is a real skill in getting the rights price spot on. The price has to be low enough to tempt shareholders to pay up but high enough to raise the amount of cash that is needed.

Underwriting a rights issue

You are *not* obliged to buy all or any of the shares offered to you in a rights issue. It is your *right* to buy, not your obligation. The rights issue may, therefore, be *underwritten*. This means that one or more stockbrokers or institutional investors have agreed to buy any shares scorned by the existing shareholders.

The underwriters will be paid a fee for their pains. After all, if the issue falls flat and few shareholders take up their rights then the underwriters will be forced to stump up the deficit. They could then be stuck with a large holding of shares that are difficult to sell.

If the company is confident of a good take-up by existing shareholders, it will not bother to have the rights issue underwritten, thus saving the cost of the underwriters' fees.

Shareholders in the company will probably be offered the opportunity to take more than their entitlement so that any rights not taken up can be distributed among those wanting extra. Otherwise any rights shares that are not applied for will be sold by the company through the stock market.

If you decline a rights offer and your entitlement is sold at a higher price than the rights price then the extra cash comes to you, minus the company's costs.

Say you are entitled to buy 1,000 shares at 100p each, that would cost you £1,000. If you forgo your rights and the shares are sold on the stock market at 150p each, the sale will raise £1,500. The company takes the £1,000 it wanted in the first place and passes the £500 'profit' to you.

It may seem a great idea to be offered cut-price shares but rights issues are not universally popular with shareholders. You may have made as big an investment as you felt comfortable with and now you are being asked to put up more cash that you may not have readily available.

Also, when a company makes a rights issue the share price tends to fall to some point between the existing share price and the rights price, so you see the value of your shareholding reduced.

Placing and open offer

Instead of giving existing share holders the right to buy new shares, a company may offer new shares to institutional investors. This is called a *placing*. Since the existing shareholders are being bypassed, they will be asked to approve this arrangement, just as they would be required to vote on a rights issue.

There are several benefits, from the company's point of view, of making a placing rather than a rights issue. First of all, it costs much less. The lower the costs of making the issue, the more of the proceeds go into the company coffers.

Offering shares to a handful of institutions, each taking a large batch of shares, is a good deal cheaper, not to mention faster, than writing to all the shareholders and allocating small parcels of shares to all those who take up the rights.

There is a greater degree of certainty in a placing. The company may already know of institutions wanting to invest.

The placing price can be decided by the company or set through what is known as *book building*. Institutions and stockbrokers will be asked how many new shares they are prepared to take and what price they are prepared to pay, so demand for shares, and the highest price that they can be sold for, is judged more accurately than taking a guess in a rights issue.

Often, though not always, a placing is accompanied by an *open offer*. This means that shareholders can apply to buy some of the shares being issued in the placing. They will pay the same price per share as the institutions.

Bonus issues and share splits

There are two other circumstances in which new shares are created but in these cases the shares are allocated automatically to the existing shareholders without payment.

Bonus issues

Under a *bonus issue*, as with a rights issue, existing shareholders will be allocated one or more shares for every so many already held. The norm is for one new share for every four or five held, although the exact proportion can vary.

Because shareholders do not have to pay anything, there is no need to apply for bonus shares. As with a rights issue, there will be a specific date on which the bonus issue will apply. Shareholders on the share register on that date get the bonus issue.

Bonus issues are usually made when a company has been trading particularly well and they frankly serve no real purpose except to provide a psychological boost by flagging up the good performance. The share price will fall in proportion to the size of the bonus issue. If you get one extra share for every five held then the share price will fall by roughly one fifth, leaving your total holding worth the same amount.

Share splits

In a *share split* the effect tends to be more dramatic. As with a bonus issue, you get extra shares free but this time you usually get far more. At the very least your shares will be split in two, so you end up with twice as many shares. If the shares are split into five you will have five shares for each one you held previously.

Again, as with the bonus issue, the share price on the stock market is likely to fall accordingly so your total holding will be worth roughly the same.

Share splits are usually introduced after a long upward run in the share price. In this country we tend to prefer share prices somewhere between 100p and 1,000p, in contrast to the US, Europe and Japan where you have fewer but more highly priced shares.

The thinking is that cheaper shares are more *marketable*. Shareholdings can be sold in smaller batches and the total price will not be so daunting for small shareholders.

This is complete nonsense. If you want to sell part but not all of your shareholding in a company you can split a batch of 100 shares into two parcels of 50 just as easily as you can split a batch of 1,000 shares into two parcels of 500 each, or 10,000 into two lots of 5,000 each.

What splitting the shares does do is to swell the size of the share register, making it more expensive to maintain. For this reason some smaller companies have resisted the convention. One example is Greggs, the bakery chain, which happily allowed its shares to rise well above 2,000p without any obvious signs of indigestion.

As with a bonus issue, a share split is usually a great psychological boost as it normally signals to the market that all is well, indeed extremely well. So while splitting the shares into, say, five should in theory reduce the price of the shares to a fifth of their former value, in practice they are likely to settle a little higher.

Companies making bonus issues or share splits will not want to suffer the ignominy of seeing the shares fall below the theoretical new price so the directors will be pretty confident about the immediate future for the company.

Case study: Rok

Rok is a property group that builds social housing, carries out construction projects and maintains buildings. After being highly successful for several years it saw its share price almost double in 2006 and stay above 1,000p in early 2007.

Rok proposed to split its shares into five, a psychological boost that pushed the share price on to 1180p by the time that shareholders approved the share split on 4th May, 2007.

In theory the shares should have opened at 236p when trading resumed after the May Bank Holiday weekend but in practice they moved to 249.5p in early deals on 8th May, effectively a gain of 13.5p.

Our table shows what happened to holdings of 1,000 shares before the share split:

Table 1: example share split

Current Situation	No. of Shares Held	Market Price	Value of Holding
Before share split	1,000	1,180p	£11,800
After share split	5,000	236p	£11,800
After share price gain	5,000	249.5p	£12,475

Vendor shares

When a company makes an *acquisition*, in other words it buys another company, it may pay cash but it may alternatively pay partly or entirely in its own shares. These are new shares issued to the owners of the company that is being bought, the vendors. You will have come across the term *vendor*, the Latin word for seller, if you have ever bought a house.

Often the vendor will give an undertaking not to sell any of the shares for a set period of time. Alternatively, the vendor may place the shares immediately with institutional investors or keep them as a long term investment.

Share options

The directors and other key executives may be awarded share options, which means they have the right to buy a set number of shares at a set price. Share option schemes are designed to provide an incentive to management.

The price the managers have to pay to buy the shares is fixed, often at quite a cheap price, so they can pocket a profit by buying the shares cheaply and selling them at a higher price. The better the company is doing, the more the shares will be worth and the bigger the profit the managers can make on their options.

Buying shares in this way is called *exercising* the options.

Secondary market

We have seen that there are various ways in which new shares are created but for the most part you will be buying shares on the secondary market, that is buying existing shares second hand. You will do this through the stock market, which we will be looking at in Section B.

It is quite likely that all the shares you ever buy will be bought on the secondary market. Certainly all the shares you ever sell will be sold on the secondary market.

The cash you pay for these shares does not go to the company. It goes to the person who already owns the shares. When you sell any shares you own, the proceeds of the sale come to you, not to the company.

Share cancellations

Shares can be cancelled as well as created. When a company is taken over, the new owners often buy all the shares from the existing shareholders and scrap the lot.

Less dramatic is the growing trend for companies to buy back some of their shares. This happens when a company has spare cash that is not needed for investment in the business. This process is often referred to as *returning cash to shareholders*, as it is the reverse of the process we have discussed in the primary market where the company issues shares to investors to raise cash.

Shares are also cancelled in a *share consolidation*. This is the reverse of a share split. A consolidation almost invariably means that the shares have sunk so low in value that they are hardly worth buying. For example, when a share price falls below the level of 1p the mechanisms for trading shares can become quite impracticable.

Say the consolidation is one share to replace every ten you already own. The hope is that the one share you now own will be priced ten times as much as each of the shares you previously held.

Unfortunately shareholders often take the opportunity of a share consolidation to sell out, so the price tends to settle below the theoretical price.

Treasury shares

Occasionally a company may buy its own shares cheaply in the hope of reissuing them later at a higher price. While these shares are held in abeyance they are known as *treasury shares*.

3.

Whose Company Is It?

The company is owned by the shareholders. Your stake in the company is in proportion to the number of shares you hold. So if you own 5% of the company you are entitled to 5% of the votes at any shareholders' meeting and also to 5% of any profit distributed as dividends.

The company will employ a firm of registrars to keep the register of shareholders up-to-date, amending the list as shares are bought and sold and mailing out the annual report and any other information that shareholders are entitled to receive.

In practice, most companies have institutional investors such as pension funds on their shareholder register and their holdings will be considerably larger than yours. They will, when things go wrong, make known their disquiet to the directors and although it may seem a little unfair that their voice is louder than yours, in most cases your interests and those of the institutions will be the same.

The directors may also sound out the views of large shareholders on a major issue such as a change of strategy or a major acquisition. It can be useful to know if a planned course of action is going to run into serious opposition.

However, companies are not allowed to give crucial information to favoured shareholders without also releasing that information to everyone through a stock exchange announcement.

The London Stock Exchange has, over the years, made valiant efforts to stamp out the issuing of inside information and the flow of information today is much, much fairer than it used to be.

The company is run on behalf of the shareholders by a board of directors. In practice, the directors tend to have a pretty free rein and, in some cases, can come to regard the company as their personal property. If it comes to a vote, though, they can be ousted by the shareholders and occasionally this does happen.

Case study: Wyevale Garden Centres

After a disappointing period of trading, Wyevale caught the attention of Laxey Partners, an investment fund that specialises in spotting underperforming companies and pressing them to buck up their ideas.

Laxey took a 28.6% stake in Wyevale in 2005 and forced an extraordinary general meeting in December 2005 at which it garnered enough support from other shareholders to vote out Wyevale chairman David Williams and two other directors.

On this occasion Laxey was supported by another investment fund, Millennium Partners, which owned 11.2% of Wyevale shares, so there was a solid block of nearly 40% of the shares in rebel hands.

Laxey failed, however, to get its own nominee, Robert Ware, the former chairman of the Stead & Simpson shoe stores chain, elected in place of Williams as many Wyevale shareholders feared that Laxey was trying to gain control of the company without making a full takeover bid.

Directors

Directors may hold shares in the company. Indeed, it is considered rather bad form if they do not as it looks like a vote of no confidence in themselves if they are not prepared to risk some of their own money in buying at least a nominal stake.

There is no set figure for how many shares a director should hold. Sometimes the entire board will hold less than 1% between them. Sometimes just one director holds more than half the shares. Factors that can affect the size of directors' shareholdings include the size of the company and whether a director has a residual holding from the days before the company was floated on the stock exchange.

Example: directors' shareholdings

As examples of directors' shareholdings, the two tables show one company where the board's holdings add up to less than 1% of the total shareholding and another where one director owns more than half the shares.

Chemring is a medium sized company supplying defence equipment such as decoys, flares and ammunition. According to its 2006 annual report, shareholdings of directors were:

Director	Position	Shares held	% of company
Kenneth Scobie	Chairman	149,864	0.5
David Price	Chief executive	36,400	0.1
Paul Rayner	Finance director	21,000	Less than 0.1%
David Evans	Non-executive	80,348	0.2%
Sir Peter Norriss	Non executive	3,600	Less than 0.1%
Ian Much	Non-executive	3,000	Less than 0.1%
Lord Freeman	Non-executive	Nil	Nil

Terrace Hill is a small property company that develops housing and commercial sites and owns offices and shopping centres as an investment. The Hemscott.com financial news website showed the following shareholdings for directors in June 2007:

Director	Position	Shares held	% of company
Robert Adair	Chairman	129,000,000	61
Philip Loooh	Managing director	1,580,000	0.8
Tom Walsh	Finance director	40,000	Less than 0.1
Robert Dyson	Non-executive	623,000	0.3
Kelvin Hudson	Non-executive	Nil	Nil
Will Wyatt	Non-executive	Nil	Nil

Any shares held by directors count equally with those held by other shareholders. A director with 5% of the shares has 5% of the votes, just as you would do with a similar stake.

There are two types of directors: *executives* and *non-executives*. They tend to sit on the *board* in roughly equal numbers but there is no set formula for how many of each a company should have.

Executive directors

The executives work for the company full-time and are responsible for the day-to-day operations. The most important executive is usually called the *chief executive*, or *group chief executive* or *chief executive officer* (CEO for short). In a smaller, privately owned company they would probably have the title *managing director*.

Whatever the actual title, this person is the top executive, the one to whom the other executives report.

After the chief executive the most prominent executive is usually the *finance director*. Other executives who may be on the board include the sales director, the marketing director and the heads of each division in the group. There will also be a company secretary who carries out certain defined legal roles. This is not always a separate post. The role could be fulfilled by, say, the finance director if the company is not large enough to justify a separate appointment.

Non-executive directors

The non-executives are part-time and may do no more than attend monthly board meetings. They are there to represent the interest of the shareholders – people like yourself. They are usually chosen for their wide business experience and their role is to offer advice and to see that the executives are doing their job.

They will probably be non-executives of several quoted companies, though they should not sit on the boards of two rival companies as there would be a clear clash of interests. They can, though, facilitate contact between two companies in which they are directors if there is a mutual advantage.

The *chairman* of the company is normally, though not always, a non-executive. He or she may well have an office at the company and perhaps work two or three days a week there, offering help and guidance to the executives as required.

The chairman chairs the board meetings, just as the chairman or woman of any formal organisation such as the Women's Institute or the British

Legion does. He or she sees that the agenda is followed, that the meeting is orderly, that all directors have their fair say and that important issues are addressed.

There is also a *vice-chairman* who is also usually non-executive and who deputises in the absence of the chairman.

The top two roles on the board are chairman and chief executive. It is regarded in the City as best practice for two separate people to hold these two roles with the chairman as a non-executive.

Occasionally one person holds both posts and we do sometimes see an executive chairman as well as a chief executive. This can cause problems over who does what and is likely to create a conflict between rival egos.

There is some kind of pecking order on the board, partly in terms of each individual's role in the company and, in the case of non-executives, based on length of service on the board.

However, it is inevitable that other factors come into play in determining whose voice carries most weight. As in all walks of life, some individuals are more ambitious than others, some are more forceful.

A chief executive who is demonstrating success in the business will command more respect than one running a struggling enterprise. Some non-executives are more adept or daring in controlling a maverick executive. Directors, in the end, are only human. Some boards pull together and others split into factions.

Directors' pay

Deciding how much the directors are paid for their services is a particularly contentious area. The board will set up a remuneration committee, probably comprising three non-executives and chaired by the longest serving one.

Executive directors will be paid for doing a full-time job, possibly quite handsomely, and there are likely to be incentives such as bonuses if certain performance targets are met. Performance targets may involve meeting minimum profit levels or raising the value of the shares on the stock market by a certain percentage.

Executives are often awarded share options, where they are allowed to buy new shares from the company cheaply or even at no cost. They will also have generous payments made into their pension fund.

Non-executives are normally paid a fixed, much lower fee, reflecting the fact that they may do no more than attend a monthly board meeting. The chairman's salary will depend on how much time he is required to spend on company business.

As a general rule, the bigger the company, the higher the remuneration for directors.

Technically, the shareholders can object to the salary structure at the annual meeting but it is extremely difficult to persuade large shareholders to make a fuss.

4.

What's In It For Me?

You've invested your money and you naturally want something in return. There are three ways you can benefit from a stock market investment:

1. dividends

2. capital gains

3. shareholder perks

Dividends

Most companies pay dividends, which come out of their profits. This is similar to receiving interest from a savings account in a bank. You get a flow of income without touching the capital invested.

If you want to invest for income, say you are retired and want to put your nest egg where it will provide you with a regular supply of cash to live on, then you will look for companies paying a dividend that is increased year by year. This is known as a *progressive dividend*.

Dividends are paid out of what are called *distributable reserves*. In simple terms, this is the pot of cash that has been built up out of the profits left over after all the bills have been paid, including tax and previous dividends.

The cash that is not distributed to shareholders in the form of a dividend is used to pay off debt, meet day-to-day bills or to fund expansion.

Companies generally aim to *cover* the dividend twice. That means that in any year they hope to earn twice as much as they pay out in the dividend.

For example, supposing a company makes £100m in profits after tax. Let us also suppose that it has 200m shares in issue, so it has earned 50p for each share (called *earnings per share*). Say it pays a dividend of 20p a share. That means the dividend is covered 2.5 times by earnings – in other words earnings are two and a half times the dividend.

These figures are purely a simple illustration. In real life they hardly ever come out in round numbers, as we can see in the table of actual examples. However, company results always include a figure for earnings per share and one for the dividend, so you can easily see whether the dividend is covered.

Table 2: sample earnings per share and dividend figures

Company	Profits After Tax	No. of Shares	Earnings Per Share	Dividend Total	Cover
Michael Page	£65.5m	334.7m	19.6p	5.3p	3.7
Whitbread	£144.5m	228.3m	63.3p	30.05p	2.1
A McAlpine	£22.8	99.9m	22.8p	14.65p	1.6
Woolworths	£13.5m	1.45m	0.9p	1.77p	0.5

There are cases, alas, when the dividend is not fully covered. In this case the company has to raid the reserves built up in the fat years as it trades through the thin ones. This cannot be done for ever, because the reserves will dwindle and when they run out it will not be legally possible to pay out any more.

If the company chooses to maintain the dividend – to pay the same amount this year as it paid last year – even though the dividend is not fully covered, it is hoping to do better in future and to restore profits to a comfortable level.

The timing of dividend payments

The dividend will be declared in pence per share, or in euros per share if the company is based in the Republic of Ireland. Most companies in this country pay dividends twice a year:

- once after the half year end (the *interim dividend*), and

- once after the financial year end (the *final dividend*).

Add the two together and you have the *total dividend* for the year.

As a rough guide, about one third of the total is usually paid out at the half way stage and two thirds after the year end. There is no set formula for this division and you should not be suspicious if a company pays the two dividends in different proportions.

There are, though, two main reasons why the interim tends to be significantly less than the final.

The company does not have a full picture of how well the year is going at the half way stage. After all, it has only half the year's figures to go on.

This is particularly true of companies that depend heavily on Christmas trading because in most cases the festive season falls in the second half of the financial year.

It is also true of holiday companies that run at a loss during the quieter winter period and make all their money in the summer sunshine. They tend to have a financial year end in September so the first half may give only a preliminary indication of how the full year will pan out. Who knows in March how many last minute bargain hunters will leap off their sofas to snap up cheap breaks?

The second reason for the smaller interim is more technical. Strictly speaking, the directors merely recommend the dividends: the payouts have to be approved by the shareholders at the annual general meeting.

You and your fellow shareholders are hardly likely to demand a smaller payout. So the directors pay the interim dividend reasonably safe in the knowledge that it will in the fullness of time be approved by the shareholders. There are no qualms about the final dividend because the annual meeting is called after the full year results are announced and the final dividend is not paid until that meeting gives the go ahead.

Just for the record, turkeys do on rare occasions vote for Christmas. There have been instances of a major shareholder arguing that it is in everyone's interest to preserve cash to develop the business for a long-term and, ultimately, a larger gain rather than pay out a smaller amount now.

A few companies pay quarterly dividends. This happens more in the US than here but larger companies with an international standing, such as oil giants BP and Shell, pay out quarterly to keep their American investors happy. The three interim payments tend to be equal instalments and the final dividend will be larger but again there is no set formula for how the total is divided.

Some smaller companies pay only one, final dividend. It is obviously twice as expensive to mail out cheques two times a year rather than just once. It may be inconvenient to wait a whole 12 months for your dividend but there is no reason to suspect the soundness of such a company. Rather, it can be a cause for rejoicing that a company with limited resources uses them prudently.

Finally, we have companies that pay no dividend at all. These are obviously of no use to you if you are looking for a stream of income from your shares unless, perhaps, there are genuine reasons to believe that a dividend is imminent.

It is possible that the directors have decided to preserve cash to use in expanding the business. More likely is that the company is loss making or has no distributable reserves so it is in no position to pay a dividend.

Note: The dates of dividend payments can usually be found in the 'investor relations' section of companies' websites.

Let us concentrate on the companies of most interest, the ones making two or four payments a year.

Dividend size

Whether payments are half-yearly or quarterly, the policy on how much to pay out at each stage remains much the same year by year at each individual company. So if the interim dividend is unchanged, it is unlikely that the final will be increased either.

On the other hand, if the interim is raised, then the company is clearly confident that the year is going well and the directors are expecting, barring any nasty surprises, to raise the final. So if the interim is raised, say, 5% you can hope that the final dividend will also go up 5%. This is *not* guaranteed, and indeed if everything goes swimmingly you might get even more, but if trading tails off in the second half you could be in for a disappointment.

Companies do occasionally *rebalance* their dividend policies. For example, directors who have been extremely cautious in setting the interim dividend in the past may feel able after a few years of strong trading to increase the interim faster than the final over one or more years to bring the ratio into line with the norm.

When a company decides to rebalance the dividend it will say so in its results statement, usually before such a change is made or possibly to explain a large dividend increase that has just been recommended.

Successful companies will have a *progressive dividend policy*, that is, the dividend will be raised every year. This is great for investors because the rising payout will offset the effects of inflation.

Not so good is when companies *rebase* their dividends. This is a euphemism for saying that the company is not making sufficient profits to justify the dividend at its current level. By setting a lower dividend for the latest financial year, the company hopes to be able to start a progressive dividend policy but from a lower level.

The following table shows a selection of dividends paid by companies of various sizes over the past five years. The dates are for the financial year to the end of March. We can see that dividends tend to rise in steady stages but they can fall sharply if profits suffer a serious setback.

Table 3: sample companies and dividend payments

Company	Business	2003	2004	2005	2006	2007
Sainsbury	Supermarket	15.4p	15.6p	13.5p	7.8p	8.25p
Majestic	Wine merchant	2.75p	4.12p	5.5p	7p	7.4p
ICI	Chemicals	6.25p	6.9p	7.65p	8.1p	9.1p
Northern Foods	Food processing	8.7p	8.9p	8.95p	9.1p	2.35p
Scottish & Southern	Energy	35p	37.7p	38.6p	44.1p	47.8p

Special dividend

Occasionally a company will pay a *special dividend*. This is usually much bigger than the interim or final. It happens when a company suddenly finds itself with more cash than it can use and the directors decide to return it to shareholders rather than leave it to gather dust in a bank account.

One instance is when a company sells a major business to another company for cash. Another possibility is that the company has been very successful and has built up a cash pile over the years. Eventually the directors realise that it does not need so much to be set aside for a rainy day.

A special dividend will usually be in addition to the interim and final dividends. This is so that the special dividend is clearly seen as a one-off. You cannot expect another special dividend in the following year.

Payment dates

When a dividend is announced the company will set two dates:

- *Qualifying date*. Shareholders on the share register on this date are entitled to receive the dividend

- *Payment date*. This is the date on which the dividend cheques are sent out.

- There is no set timeframe for dividend payments. Some companies pay within a few weeks of declaring the dividend; others wait months.

Up to the qualifying date the shares will be bought and sold *cum dividend*. That means with the dividend. If you sell shares at this stage the right to receive the dividend passes to the buyer.

Ultimately the day arrives when the company pays up and the shares go *ex dividend*, that is without the dividend. (You learn Latin reading this book as well as maths!) Now you keep the dividend if you sell the shares and you are not entitled to it if you buy the shares.

When shares go ex dividend, the price will fall to reflect that fact that the buyer will not get the payout. This fall will be roughly equivalent to the size of the dividend.

Four large companies from different sectors went ex dividend on Wednesday, 4 April 2007. The following table shows the size of the dividend paid and the movement in the share price that day.

Table 4: sample companies and dividend payments

Company	Dividend	Share Price	Effective Change
Alliance & Leicester	36.5p	- 38p	- 1.5p
Pearson	17p	- 19p	- 2p
Kingfisher	6.8p	- 5p	+ 1.8p
Hanson	15.35p	- 15.5p	- 0.15p

Shares were generally little changed that day, with the Footsie adding just 4 points.

Three of the four shares featured fell by more than the dividend. Pearson would have been expected to lose 17p, since anyone buying the shares at that point would not get the 17p final dividend for the 2006 financial year. In the event the shares lost 19p, a fall of an extra 2p.

In contrast, Kingfisher eased only 5p despite the loss of a 6.8p dividend to anyone buying the shares on that day.

The shares will go cum dividend then ex dividend every time that the company declares and pays a dividend.

Capital gains

You may be more interested in seeing the value of your shares rise than in receiving a steady stream of income. In that case you will be looking for companies that you feel are undervalued by other investors and whose share prices will rise as other investors catch on. You want to get in first.

The money you invest is referred to as *capital* and any increase in its value is a *capital gain*.

Having it both ways

You can have the best of both worlds by investing in companies that see their share prices rise as the dividend goes up. In fact, you may ask, surely the two go together.

Indeed, you may see an ideal investment as one where the profits rise year by year, the dividend paid out of those profits similarly rises, making the shares more attractive, so more investors want to buy and the share price goes up further.

Quite right. Profits, dividends and share prices often do move in the same direction in roughly equal measure.

Do remember, though, that the stock market rarely moves in symmetrical ways. Some companies may pay more out in dividends while others retain the cash for expansion. A company that has made heavy losses in the past may seem a worthwhile investment now it is making profits but it may have no reserves left to pay a dividend.

Shareholder perks

A minority of companies offer shareholders discounts off their products or services. These include jewellery, clothing, food and drink, air fares, new and used cars and magazines.

For example, Eurotunnel offered its original shareholders three free trips through the Chunnel each year, while various housebuilders have offered thousands of pounds off one of their new homes.

These perks can look very attractive but there are several disadvantages—

1. Most obviously, if you do not want to travel by car to France or buy a new home from a particular builder then the concession is of no use to you. There is no point in buying shares at Moss Bros if you get your suits at Marks & Spencer.

2. A minimum shareholding is often required to qualify for the perk. Although in some companies just one share is sufficient, others reserve the benefit for holders of at least 2,500 shares.

3. Companies may require investors to hold the shares for a minimum period, usually one year but sometimes longer.

4. Perks can be withdrawn or changed so it is difficult to keep track of what is currently available. Some companies notify the shareholders about what perks are offered in the annual report so you have to buy the shares first and find out your entitlement later.

When you are paid cash as a dividend you can spend the money as you please. But with perks you are stuck with what you are given.

The following table shows a selection of the perks that have been available in the past, but investors will need to check with individual companies to ensure that the concessions still exist.

Table 5: sample companies and perks offered to shareholders

Company	Sector	Perk	Minimum shareholding
Persimmon	Housebuilder	£3,000 off new home	1,000 shares
Signet	Jewellers	10% discount	1 share
British Airways	Airline	10% discount	100 shares
Wolves & Dudley	Pubs	20% discount	10 shares

5.

Is My Investment Safe?

Imagine walking into a bookmakers and finding that most horses won, often at pretty decent odds. Or visiting a casino where there is no zero on the roulette wheel and the dealer's blackjack cards are dealt face up.

Welcome to the world of the stock market.

Yes, it is a gamble picking shares but it is one where the odds are stacked in favour of the punters, where the majority walk out winners instead of losers.

Shares do represent a riskier investment than putting your money into a savings account with a fixed rate of interest but the risk is much less than you think and the potential rewards are much greater.

Sure, if you put away a large enough sum of money into a savings account you might be able to live off the interest – for now. But your savings are being eaten away all the time by inflation. As the years go by, that fixed rate of interest is worth less and less while your lump sum never increases.

By contrast, dividends on shares generally rise over the years to offset inflation and, over time, most shares increase in value.

Every investor needs a well balanced portfolio of about 10-12 shares spread across different sectors such as a bank, a house builder, a power company, a transport provider and so on. So if one share suffers, the likelihood is that the others will compensate.

Yes, it is possible for the whole market to tumble, as it did between 2000 and 2003, but even if you bought right at the top of the market in March 2000 and clung on obstinately you would still probably be better off today than if you had let your cash dwindle away in the bank or building society.

In that sense, investing in the stock market is safer than a savings account. And you can decide for yourself how much risk you want to take. Do you go for big solid household names or pick out up-and-coming young companies? By learning how the market operates and how to avoid pitfalls you can learn to take sensible decisions to create a portfolio that suits you.

It is true that there are unscrupulous people in the stock market as there are in any walk of life. Shares often move before a big announcement as those in the know buy or sell before the rest of the market catches on. Insider trading is virtually impossible to stamp out entirely.

However, there are three different bodies policing UK stock market investments with considerable effect.

London Stock Exchange (LSE)

First, there is the *London Stock Exchange*. It has strict rules on when directors can buy or sell shares in their own company and on when they must alert the market to a change in profit expectations. All formal announcements on matters such as takeovers and mergers, results and major transactions must be made publicly at the earliest opportunity. In practice, such statements are almost invariably issued through the London Stock Exchange itself.

Takeover Panel

Then there is the *Takeover Panel*, whose job is to ensure fair play not only in takeovers but also in mergers and when large investors take major stakes in a company. The Panel oversees the Takeover Code, which sets a timetable for bids, decides when control has passed to a new owner and determines what the various parties to a bid can say and do.

Above all, the Panel ensures that all shareholders great and small must be treated equally in a takeover.

Financial Services Authority (FSA)

Finally, the *Financial Services Authority* has an overall responsibility for regulating the entire financial services sector, including stock market dealings. It can investigate suspicious trades and fine companies and individuals who do not play the game.

However, in the final resort it is up to you to go into stock market investing with your eyes open, to do your homework and to know what you are doing. Do not expect some fairy godmother to step forward and make up your losses. After all, you expect to pocket any gains you make, so pay up if you get it wrong. The stock market is not for wimps.

Shares versus other investments

Other forms of investment apart from savings accounts can make you money. Gold has on occasions proved a good short term bet. Rare stamps, paintings, coins, wine, even carpets have their day. Indeed, in the past tulip bulbs presented one of Europe's most notorious boom and bust stories.

As with your house, with shares, with the contents of your attic, what you own is worth what someone else is prepared to pay. And if the price of a case of 1996 Latour or an 1882 British Empire Orange stamp starts to motor then other investors are sucked in until the bubble bursts.

Stocks, too, can be subject to the vagaries of passing whims, as first biotechs and then computer technology shares have demonstrated in recent years. The big safeguard with shares is that unless you take silly risks on ephemeral fancies you are buying a stake in something that has a real value of its own. For as long as the goods the company makes or the services it provides have value, then the company and its shares have value.

Shares are linked to the health of UK and overseas economies. The amount of goods and services sold rises as economies grow and falls in recession. The fact is that economies around the world spend longer growing than contracting. The world is, overall, a richer place than it was 10, 20, 50 or 100 years ago.

By investing in shares, you take your stake in the increasing wealth of the UK and the world.

If inflation is only 2.5%, then £10,000 falls in value to £9,750 over the course of just one year and to £8,810 in five years. If inflation is 5%, then your £10,000 is halved in less than 15 years. So you have to constantly top up your savings account out of the interest you receive just to maintain the real value of your savings. It is like running to stand still.

Shares on average not only keep pace with inflation, they provide you with an income as well.

There have been periods when shares have fallen over several months, even over years. The FTSE lost three quarters of its value in 1973-74. In 2000 we launched on a decline that was not quite so steep – the FTSE 100 lost over half its value – but it was a much longer downward grind lasting three years.

However, shares gain in value in far more years than they fall.

Chart 1: UK stock market compared to gold

The chart shows the general performance of the UK stock market since 1970 – with, for comparison, the performance of gold over the same period.

The one other alternative form of investment that combines income with rising values is property. There has over the past few years been a boom in buy-to-let, purchasing houses to rent out. As with shares, values can fall as well as rise but they rise more years than they fall.

Property does involve administration and maintenance. While you can decline to commit more cash in a rights issue, you cannot ignore a leaky roof whether you have the cash to fix it or not.

Insider trading

Small investors may have been justifiably alarmed to read an admission by the Financial Services Authority early in 2007 that insider trading happens ahead of nearly one in four takeovers.

The evidence is that 24% of target companies in 2005 saw their share price rise before they revealed that they had received an approach. The previous year had been even worse at 32%, almost one third of all takeovers on the London Stock Exchange.

Insider trading is pernicious and the authorities here have been criticised for failing to attack it in the way that the US authorities tackle white collar crime. There has been just one successful case for market abuse brought in the UK in recent years.

However, it will be impossible to stamp the practice out entirely as long as greed is one of the seven deadly sins.

While this is a matter for concern, we need to get it in proportion. Unless you bought shares just before the approach was revealed, or intended to buy shares but were put off by the share price increase, you have not been affected adversely. Only those who paid over the odds for their shares or who missed out on a short term profit have cause to complain.

If you already held the shares, then you benefited from the share price increase.

Because companies are obliged to issue a public statement when there is a sharp movement in their share price, we are talking about a very short time frame, possibly just the first hour of trading when most private investors are inactive. Once the news is out in the open, the shares would rise anyway.

Companies that have received a takeover approach are expected to do the decent thing and inform the market as soon as there is any reasonable prospect of a firm offer emerging.

However, the Takeover Code explicitly acknowledges the obvious fact that a company may not be aware that it is being eyed up as a bid target and it cannot be expected to disclose something it does not know about yet.

Nor do companies need to reveal every single conversation they have with a potential bidder. One might argue that all approaches should be revealed immediately but that would be quite impracticable and would do more harm than good.

Many approaches come to nothing so there is no point in boosting bid hopes prematurely. As it is, many approaches are rejected without being translated into a firm proposal or the potential bidder decides it is not worth pressing its case.

However, target companies are required to do the decent thing and own up if their share price starts to rise while secret talks are going on to nip any insider trading in the bud.

Insider trading can also happen ahead of the announcement of better or worse than expected company results. Here the authorities have been much more successful in stamping out the insider trading that was once widespread. According to FSA figures, only about 2% of company results are preceded by inspired buying or selling of the shares, a big improvement over the past decade.

Companies have become far more responsible in keeping investors informed of any changes in trading conditions and they are certainly required to alert the stock market to any substantial changes in profit expectations, whether for better or worse.

THE STOCK MARKET | B

6.

The Market Place

The stock market, like any market, is where you buy and sell new and second hand goods, in this case shares in a company. Companies willingly pay a fee for a stock market listing because it is easier to persuade investors to buy shares if they can be sold easily at a later date.

Shares do not have to be traded on a stock market. Supposing you have a bright idea but you do not have the cash needed to make and market the wonderful gizmo that you have invented. You ask your Grandma, or Auntie Maisie, or the neighbours, anyone who believes in you to put up the cash in return for a stake in the rewards when your great invention starts to sell like hot cakes.

Alas, Grandma dies, you fall out with Auntie Maisie and your neighbours move to the Outer Hebrides and the cash has to be repaid just when you need it most. Wouldn't it be so much better if new investors stepped forward to buy the stakes of those who want out? If your shares are traded on the stock market, that is exactly what happens.

What is more, people will be far more willing to put their faith and their life savings into your venture if they have the reassurance of knowing that, should they want to get out, they can do so readily.

The stock market provides the reassurance that it will bring together buyers and sellers on a trading platform where the price of the transaction will be set according to supply and demand.

7.

London Stock Exchange

The main exchange for trading shares in this country is the London Stock Exchange (LSE). It was the first stock exchange to be set up and it remains one of the three most prestigious in the world alongside the New York Stock Exchange in the US and the Tokyo Stock Exchange in Japan.

Because these three exchanges are in different time zones, it means that from the opening in Tokyo to the close in New York there is a major stock market open somewhere for most hours of most weekdays.

In addition to UK companies, about 350 overseas companies from more than 50 countries have their share prices quoted on the LSE to gain access to the finance they need to flourish.

The total number of companies quoted on the LSE is approaching 3,000 and they are worth in total well over £3,500 billion.

A London listing gives these companies from across the globe prestige. They are attracted by the *liquidity* of the London market and the balance that we have here between encouraging entrepreneurial spirit and imposing sufficient sensible regulation to retain the confidence of investors and quoted companies alike.

Liquidity refers to how active the market is. The more buyers and sellers there are for a company's shares, and the more trading that takes place, the more *liquid* those shares are. They flow readily. If trading is active, investors are willing to buy because they know they will have no difficulty in selling whenever they want to.

History of the Exchange

The London Stock Exchange began with brokers meeting in London coffee houses way back in the 18th century. Indeed, it can be argued that the issuing of a list of stock and commodity prices in 1698 is the earliest evidence of organised stock market trading in the world.

The dealers had to meet in coffee houses at first because their behaviour was too rowdy for the liking of the Royal Exchange, where other commodities were traded.

The first stock exchange premises were established in 1761 and when formal membership, by subscription, was instituted in 1801, the modern stock exchange where members could trade with each other was born. Eleven years later a rule book was created.

It took until 1973 for the first female members to be admitted and in the same year the regional stock exchanges that had sprung up in cities beginning with Manchester and Liverpool were amalgamated into one national exchange.

Big Bang

Since then modernisation has snowballed in the electronic age. Deregulation of the market, known as *Big Bang*, took place in 1986.

Until then, trading had been a highly complex business full of restrictive practices such as being able to charge investors minimum rates of commission. Although investors placed their buy and sell orders with stock brokers, these orders had to be relayed to *jobbers* on the stock exchange floor. Errors could occur as jobbers misunderstood each other's orders or scribbled down the wrong details in the hurly-burly of the trading floor.

Everything had to be matched up at the end of the day and disputes were settled by an independent committee.

Brokers and, in particular, the jobbers who saw their jobs disappearing, forecast that Big Bang would be the end of the world but in many ways it was the start of the LSE as we now know it.

All member firms became broker-dealers, able to take orders and do the actual buying and selling. Minimum commission rates were abolished, so private investors were encouraged to place orders because they now paid lower charges.

The old octagonal stock exchange building was situated just round the corner from the Bank of England in the main part of London's financial centre known as the City. It used to be buzzing with brokers, jobbers, traders and investors.

Now trading is carried out mostly on silent computer screens in offices scattered around the globe rather than face to face on a market floor and the LSE has moved into smaller new headquarters in Paternoster Square close to St Paul's Cathedral.

The Stock Exchange Electronic Trading Service (SETS), has been established to make trading instantaneous and Crest, an automatic settlement service, clears shares and payments electronically without the need for paper.

Trading hours

The London Stock Exchange operates within set hours. At 7am the formal announcements lodged overnight while the exchange was closed start to pour out. The intention is to give everyone an equal opportunity to trade on a fair basis. Announcements will continue to be made throughout the day but the overwhelming majority come out as the market opens.

In theory we therefore all start trading on an equal footing. Yes, the professionals in the City are going to be at their desks and ahead of the average punter first thing in a morning so you will, in practice, find that share prices often move before you have a chance to react. However, at least there is some attempt to create a level playing field.

Trading in smaller shares starts at 7am. Those in larger companies do not start until 8pm, after the London Stock Exchange has run a complex computer program through to match up any attempted trades left over from the previous night.

Trading then continues right through the lunch hour until 4.30pm.

Announcements continue to be issued until 6.30pm. Most after-hours statements cover directors' share dealings but occasionally a profit warning is slipped out, perhaps in the hope that the press won't notice. (The press always *do* notice and in consequence this underhand practice is far less common than it used to be).

Summary of Exchange trading hours

Time	Event
7am	Trading in smaller shares starts Formal news announcements start
8am	Trading in main shares starts
4.30pm	Close of trading
6.30pm	Formal news announcements end

News announcements

The overwhelming majority of announcements are made through the London Stock Exchange's Regulatory News Service (RNS). This used to be compulsory but other news distributors are now allowed to compete provided they make the information widely available to newspapers, to wire services such as the Press Association and to financial news websites. The aim is to widely spread the news to all investors as quickly as possible.

News that has not been released in this way does sometimes leak out into the newspapers. The powers that be discourage this practice. In particular, the 'Friday night drop' in which financial advisers slipped out tasty morsels to favoured Sunday newspaper journalists after the market had closed for the week has been stamped out.

However, where news genuinely occurs after the stock market has closed, it is permissible for companies to release the information to the press provided at least two newspapers or news agencies such as the Press Association or Reuters are informed.

Curiously, the tipping off of scribes on the Financial Times, the newspaper read by City professionals on their way to the office, has never been attacked by financial regulators with the same zeal as leaks to lesser publications.

Do not be too angry that the professionals have a built in advantage. Share prices can be erratic first thing in a morning and unsuspecting private investors who instruct their stockbrokers to buy or sell at the best available price as soon as the market opens often strike a worse deal than they expect.

If you miss an opportunity, learn to live with it and move on. There are plenty more investments to be made.

8.

Full Listings And AIM

The London Stock Exchange (LSE) does not have the right to a monopoly on share trading. Indeed, in the past there were several stock exchanges in large cities around the UK. Today, although the LSE is by far the largest stock exchange in the UK, it does face some competition from smaller exchanges setting up, not to mention competition from overseas stock exchanges.

One of the smaller exchanges is called Plus, formerly known as Ofex. This market is not part of the LSE and the regulations governing companies whose shares are quoted on Plus are less rigorous. It tends to cater for very small, comparatively new companies.

All companies whose shares are traded on the LSE market are known as *quoted companies* (alternatively it can be said that they have a *stock market quotation*).

There are two sections to the LSE, the main board and the Alternative Investment Market (AIM). Strictly speaking only companies on the main board are said to be *listed* although the term is now widely used to also describe AIM companies.

Full listing

Most of the biggest companies in the country, and many foreign ones, have their shares traded on what is known as the *main board* (even if share prices are no longer stuck up on a board in a trading room in the exchange).

This is referred to as a *full listing*. Listed companies must abide by certain rules which are designed to protect investors, such as:

- Newly listed companies must have a record of trading successfully for the previous five years.

- Listed companies must issue financial results twice a year within a set time.

- They must issue a warning if profits are likely to fall substantially short of expectations, or alert investors if they are doing considerably better than anyone thought likely.

- Directors are allowed to buy or sell shares in their own company only at specified times when all relevant news is known to everyone. They cannot, for example, trade just before results are announced – the *close period* – or when they know that any information that could influence the price of their shares is to be issued.

- Companies must hold an annual meeting at which all shareholders are entitled to attend.

The LSE charges companies a fee for the right to have shares listed on the main board. While this is no problem to giants such as BP or Vodafone, the cost can be onerous for smaller companies. Also there may be worthy companies that fall a little way short of the requirements for a full listing.

So the LSE runs a second trading board called the *Alternative Investment Market* (usually referred to by its initials *AIM*).

Alternative Investment Market

AIM has been an amazing success story since it was established in 1995 with just a handful of companies traded and it has now attracted well over 1,000 companies whose shares were worth about £40bn in aggregate in mid-2007.

The fees are lower on AIM than for a full listing so it is ideal for newer, growing businesses. The rules are a little laxer, although they still offer protection to shareholders.

Some companies want their shares to be quoted on AIM in the hope that one day they will grow up and join the big boys on the main board. Others, such as Monsoon, Domino's Pizza and Majestic Wine, are happy to be quoted on AIM, although they have the size for a full listing if they so wished, while some companies, such as housebuilder Abbey, used to have a full listing but have moved to AIM for the looser regulation and to save money.

The chart below shows the performance of AIM stocks relative to stocks with a full listing – the greater volatility of the former can easily be seen.

Chart 2: AIM v FT All Share Index

Just as the main board is the premier stock market in Europe, AIM is the most prestigious market for smaller companies in Europe and it is rapidly gaining a worldwide reputation, attracting emerging Chinese companies anxious to raise Western capital to offset the lack of investment funds at home.

Regulation

The requirements for a quotation on AIM are minimal. There is no minimum size for companies joining; no minimum percentage of shares that must be in public hands; no trading record is needed; and there is no requirement for companies to be incorporated in the UK.

Approval of shareholders is not required for most transactions.

The one major requirement is that companies must have a *nominated adviser* (or *nomad* for short). The nomad must be approved by the LSE – currently the list runs to about 80 – and actually has to meet more requirements than the AIM-quoted company itself. The nomad is responsible to the exchange for assessing that the company is suitable for AIM and for advising and guiding the company on its responsibilities.

If an AIM company falls out with its nomad and suddenly finds itself without one the exchange will suspend trading in its shares. Failure to find a replacement nomad means expulsion from AIM.

AIM companies must also have a stockbroker to ensure that there is a market in the company's shares. The nomad usually acts as broker.

Although joining AIM may look easy, quoted companies are required to play fair, for example:

- They must inform shareholders, through the LSE, of any changes in their financial condition such as increasing their bank loans or failing to pay them when due.

- They must alert the market immediately if they realise that their business has taken a distinct turn for the better or for the worse and if profits are likely to beat expectations or to fall short.

- Any change in the nature of the business must be disclosed, including plans to acquire another company or to sell part of the existing business.

In short, an AIM company must speak up if it knows of anything not yet in the public domain that would substantially affect the share price when it leaks out.

The LSE has powers to discipline AIM companies that get out of line. It can issue a warning, a fine or a censure and, in the last resort, can throw the company out. Nomads tend to take these disciplinary actions as seriously as the companies they advise, since it affects their reputation.

AIM companies must publish their interim and full year results within four months of the period end.

Directors cannot buy or sell shares in their own company for up to two months before results are announced, or at any time when they are in possession of price sensitive information that has not yet been published. For example, they cannot dump some of their shares on the market when they know they are about to issue a profit warning.

From an investor's point of view there are advantages and disadvantages in buying shares on the main board or AIM.

Capital gains tax is levied on profits from selling shares on the main board; shares in AIM companies are treated as unquoted and capital gains tax is reduced.

Tax

Most AIM stocks are exempt from inheritance tax after they have been held for two years. Those that do not are land and property; financial activities including banking and insurance; legal services and accountancy; farming and forestry; and managing hotels and nursing homes. The list could change at the whim of the Chancellor of the Exchequer.

This exemption is, admittedly a benefit for your heirs rather than for you but it is worth remembering in these days when avoiding inheritance tax has become a national sport and all the other obvious loopholes have been closed by Chancellors of the Exchequer in successive Budgets.

Note that Gordon Brown hinted at the possible removal of this benefit when he raised the Inheritance Tax threshold in his 2007 Budget. Although he will not be around at No. 11 Downing Street to withdraw the perk, the door has been opened for his successor to do so.

Already the Chancellor gets his revenge by refusing to let you put AIM stocks into ISAs or PEPs, the tax-free investment schemes.

This can be particularly inconvenient if you have in your ISA a main board company that decides to move down to AIM. When a company announces its intention to move down to AIM you are likely to see heavy selling, not only from ISA holders but also from investment funds that specifically invest only in full listings.

Suspension of share trading

Companies can have trading of their shares suspended or even cancelled for breaches of rules, though the LSE is reluctant to take such drastic steps unless necessary as it punishes the innocent shareholders, who are then locked in to holding shares that cannot be sold, along with the errant directors.

The most likely reason for a suspension is a failure to produce interim or full year results within the specified time of four months.

Most companies failing this requirement tend to comply within days but longer suspensions have been known. There is no limit to the length of time that a company can be suspended on the main board but AIM companies are automatically struck off after six months.

Examples of shares being suspended include:

- Interactive Gaming, an online sports betting and gaming operator, failed to produce its audited accounts to 31 November, 2006, within six montsh and its shares were suspended on AIM on 1 June 2007. Share trading was restored on 26 June, 2007, when the results were issued.

- China Wonder, a manufacturer of packaging machinery, was suspended on 1 June 2007 when its nominated adviser and broker Blue Oar Securities resigned. WH Ireland was appointed as a replacement a month later and share trading resumed.

- Bright Futures turned itself into a cash shell in April 2006 when it sold all its operations. Under AIM rules, inactive companies are suspended after 12 months and this happened on 2 April 2007.

We should note that companies can ask for trading in their shares to be suspended pending an important announcement. This may be a sizeable acquisition or possibly a takeover of the company.

Where the dreaded phrase 'pending clarification of the company's financial position' is attached to the notice of suspension, investors should fear the worst. It usually means that the company has run out of cash and can't persuade its bankers to put up any more.

Usually, but mercifully not always. Sometimes it really does mean that the financial position is being sorted out.

9.

How Shares Are Traded

When share trading started in the coffee houses of London in the 17th century investors would have met face to face to make deals. However, the system became increasingly impractical as the number of investors and companies grew. This was the beginning of stock exchanges, which grew up around the country. It was found more efficient for all interested investors to meet in one designated exchange where the best prices could be found in an ordered market.

Over time a system developed where investors gave their orders to *stockbrokers*, who in turn dealt with *jobbers* on an exchange. The jobbers would ensure the smooth functioning of the market by always offering to buy or sell shares – *at a price*. This system worked fine for a couple of centuries, until towards the end of the 20th century when advances in technology and finance sparked a revolution in how shares were traded.

Different forms of trading

Because companies of all sorts and sizes seek to have their shares quoted on the stock market, the London Stock Exchange has created different trading platforms (different ways in which buy and sell orders are matched up).

These are based on how liquid the shares are. Liquidity refers to how active trading in a particular share is. The most liquid shares, such as those in HSBC, BP or Vodafone, see a trade go through every few seconds throughout the day. *Illiquid* shares may see a whole day go by without a single deal being struck.

Shares in smaller companies may be illiquid, in other words there are fewer buyers and sellers around, perhaps because there are fewer shares in issue, or the company is little known and does not attract the interest of investors, or perhaps large blocks of shares are in the hands of a few major investors who rarely sell.

While AIM stocks tend on the whole to be smaller and less liquid than those on the main board, we are seeing increasingly that shares at the top end of AIM are larger and more liquid than fledgling stocks on the main board.

Different trading systems have evolved out of the cumbersome trading methods used before Big Bang catapulted the City into the emerging electronic age.

In the past, investors placed their buy orders with a stockbroker, who carried out the requests through a jobber, who carried out the actual trade on the trading room floor by finding another jobber trying to sell a similar amount of the same shares at roughly the same price at pretty much the same time.

It was an expensive, time consuming and not altogether satisfactory way of doing business in the modern era, though you had probably guessed that already.

Trading now is carried out on computer screens among stockbrokers and other serious traders willing to pay for the privilege of access to the London Stock Exchange's trading system.

Market makers

Initially after Big Bang all shares had *market makers*. These were stockbrokers willing to guarantee to buy or sell shares in a particular company. They posted their buy and sell prices on the stock exchange's electronic system.

Market makers still create a market in illiquid stocks, ensuring that there is always a buyer and a seller available. If there are no investors wanting to buy, the market maker acts as the buyer. If there are no sellers, the market maker acts as the seller.

At any given time, market makers will have a batch of shares of each company on their books so that they can fulfil any buy orders. The precise number of shares will vary from day to day depending on whether they have fulfilled more buying or more selling orders that day.

Because there are more than 2,000 companies quoted on the London Stock Exchange, market makers are not expected to make markets in all of them. It would tie up an enormous amount of cash holding shares in them all. It would also involve an excessive number of staff adjusting share prices in every single company to keep the book balanced.

Instead, market makers are allowed to stipulate which companies they will make markets in on the strict understanding that they must fulfil their obligation throughout stock market trading hours.

When a buy order comes in, market makers fulfil the order then raise their prices to attract sellers and deter further buying. They hope to balance their books, buying and selling roughly equal numbers of shares in each company each day. Getting the balance right is a skilled job.

Market makers quote a *spread*, a gap between the buying and selling prices. This provides them with a profit to cover their costs and also with a cushion in case the share price moves.

Where there is more than one market maker in a particular stock, they will quote similar but not necessarily identical prices for that stock. For illustration, let us say that four market makers in Widgets UK were quoting a buy price of 102p and a sell price of 98p. The spread for each market maker would be 98-102p.

Broker A might fulfil a buy order and move its spread up to 99p-103p. One of Broker B's clients wants to sell, so after doing the business Broker B moves its quote to 97-101p.

It would now be possible to sell at 99p at Broker A or buy at 101p at Broker B provided you went to the right broker in each case. The narrower gap of 99-101p is known as the *touch*, which is the narrowest gap between the available buying and selling prices.

The problem is that market makers must keep enough shares on their books to be able to meet orders but not so many that they get caught with heavy losses if the share price falls.

Inevitably it can happen that occasionally market makers get caught out and find themselves scrambling round to buy or sell shares where there had been heavy demand. This causes more volatility in the share price movement. However, this system proved to be a big improvement on what went before.

Let us now look at the London Stock Exchange's computerised trading systems that have evolved since market makers emerged from Big Bang.

SETS

The largest companies on the London Stock Exchange, including all the 100 biggest ones and the most actively traded medium sized ones, trade on SETS, the electronic order book. This is the most up-to-date of the trading systems and by far the most efficient and open in matching buyers and sellers.

If you want to buy, your broker will post your bid price and the number of shares you are looking for onto the trading system from its office computer. If you want to sell, your offer price and number of shares for sale are similarly posted.

When a buyer and a seller post the same price, the two are automatically matched up. If, say, the buyer wants 2,000 shares and the seller is offering 3,000 shares, the deal is struck for 2,000 shares (the lower figure) and a sale offer for 1,000 shares remains on the computer system.

Anyone with access to the trading system – and even a private investor can see the prices displayed on several financial websites for a subscription fee – is able to see not only the best buying and selling prices available but also how many buy or sell orders have been posted and at what prices.

A clear picture can thus be gained of whether one side outnumbers the other and the sort of levels at which buyers would start to bail out if the share price rises, or where supporters would pile in if the price falls.

There is a hybrid system called *SETSmm* where the electronic order book is supported by market making so that buy and sell prices are available to investors in medium sized and many smaller stocks.

If trading in a company on SETSmm dries up at any time, market makers will guarantee to buy and sell your shares at the prices they post on screen.

All medium sized companies that are not traded on SETS, the more liquid of the smaller companies on the main board and the more liquid AIM stocks, qualify for SETSmm.

Irish companies quoted in London as well as Dublin are traded on SETSmm.

SEAQ

About 2,000 smaller UK companies on the main market and AIM are traded on Seaq. This trading platform is for companies that are not sufficiently liquid to be traded on SETS because there would be times when no buy or sell offers were posted and trading would grind to a halt.

Instead, at least two market makers guarantee to post buy and sell prices throughout stock exchange trading hours.

SEATS Plus

This service covers the least liquid stocks on the main market and on AIM, where there is only one market maker or possibly none. Either the market maker will be obliged to quote buy and sell prices or your broker will take your order and try to match it with an opposite buy or sell order placed by another investor. This is the only type of deal on the stock exchange now that is order driven rather than price driven.

Share certificates and Crest

Shareholders have traditionally held pieces of paper called *share certificates* that record the name of the company whose shares were bought and the number of shares held. Under this arrangement you hand your share certificate back to the broker so that it can be cancelled and a new certificate is issued to the person buying the shares from you.

But this is a cumbersome system. It can take several days for the paperwork to be done and the certificate to be delivered to the new shareholder. Certificates may get lost and without them you cannot prove you own the shares. Replacement certificates can be issued but you have to pay the cost of producing them. In short, the system is awkward, time-consuming and expensive.

To improve matters, the London Stock Exchange has set up an electronic settlement service, called *CREST*, so that share sales and purchases can be recorded more easily and more quickly. Investors who fear the electronic world of the 21st century can be assured that this system does work. It was heavily tested over many months before it was launched and share registers were added one or two at a time, starting with the largest companies, so the system was never overloaded.

Shares held in the CREST system are referred to as being in *dematerialised* or *electronic* form. That just means they are not printed on paper.

One drawback of CREST is that shares are normally held by your stockbroker shares in a *nominee account,* that is an account in the broker's name. The broker has already paid for the right to make transactions through CREST and can easily set up a nominee account for all your transactions, which are kept separate from the broker's other clients.

Unfortunately that means you lose your rights as a shareholder, as the shares will be recorded on the share register in the broker's name, not yours.

You can ask the broker to register shares cleared through CREST in your own name in order to retain your rights to have accounts posted to your home address and to vote at shareholder meetings, but you will have to pay a fee for the privilege. Charges vary so ask your broker how much it will cost.

Whichever system you use for buying and selling shares, any deal you make takes place immediately, irrespective of how long the deal takes to be processed.

10.

Stock Market Indices

It is quite easy to watch the progress of one or two shares day by day but you cannot possibly spot all the movements of all the shares on the London Stock Exchange.

It can, though, be useful to keep track of how the market generally is faring, so you can tell whether your shares are doing better than average or you can watch for warning signs that the market is weak. So a series of stock market indices has been devised which can tell you how the whole market or various parts of it have moved overall during the day.

Each index is calculated as a figure and the size of the change in that figure reflects the scale of the movement of the market as a whole.

On any trading day, some shares rise, others fall and some stand still. Stock market indices average out the changes to give a representative overall picture. Changes are calculated moment by moment, each change in any share price being reflected automatically calculated by computer.

These changes can be recorded on a chart, just as movements of an individual share price are.

Some indices cover companies of a specific size, such as the largest, the medium sized ones or just the tiniest. Others comprise specific *sectors*, that is all the companies in a particular line of businesses. For example, there are separate indices covering oil and gas, industrials, telecoms and utilities.

Then there are indices for sub-sectors. For instance, as well as an index covering all financial companies there is an index comprising banks, one for life insurance and another for general insurers.

Meet the Footsie family

While the FTSE 100 index, covering the biggest companies listed on the London Stock Exchange, is the Daddy of them all, there's a whole range of little 'footsies' dancing around to help you to see in which direction the stock market is really running.

FTSE stands for Financial Times Stock Exchange. A joint committee from the newspaper and the exchange decide which companies go into which index. They meet every three months, early in March, June, September and December, always on a Wednesday.

Which companies go into which index will depend on share prices at the close of trading on the previous evening. Any agreed changes will take effect over the weekend that falls 10 days later, so some companies will end the week in one index and start the next week, somewhere round about the 20th day of the month, with a new status.

FTSE 100

The FTSE 100, the one usually referred to affectionately as the *Footsie*, is intended to cover the 100 companies with the largest stock market capitalisations (usually abbreviated to *market cap*). The capitalisation of a company is the value that the stock market puts on the entire company and is calculated by multiplying the share price by the number of shares that have been issued.

The committee does have some leeway is deciding membership of the FTSE 100, otherwise the index would have companies bobbing in and out every quarter.

The top 90 companies must be included. Any company ranked lower than 110 must be excluded. The committee decides which of the 20 companies in between are in and which are out.

The main consideration is stability. Companies already in the top flight will normally be retained even if they slip just outside the top 100 on the day that the axe happens to fall. A company that looks as if it is here to stay will take precedence over one that could be a flash in the pan.

Chart 3: FTSE 100 Index

FTSE 250

Immediately below the FTSE 100 is the FTSE 250, which covers the next 250 medium sized companies. This is often referred to as the *midcap* index, the one covering shares with middle-sized capitalisations.

Into this index go all those shares that narrowly missed the FTSE 100 and, again, the committee has discretion over which of the borderline cases are included at the bottom end.

Chart 4: FTSE 250 Index

Comparing the above chart of the FTSE 250 Index with that of the FTSE 100 Index it is not easy to see which index has been the stronger performer. This can be seen better in the following chart, where the two indices have been re-based to start at 100 (a common technique used to compare the performance of two or more stocks or indices.

Chart 5: FTSE 100 Index v FTSE 250 Index

It can be seen that up to 2003 the two indices tracked each other very closely, but since then the FTSE 250 Index has greatly out-performed the FTSE 100 Index. In practical terms this means that investing in a broad range of middle-capitalised stocks (i.e. medium-sized companies) would have made more money than investing in large companies since 2003.

FTSE 350

These two indexes are combined in the FTSE 350 index comprising the 350 largest companies. This is an often ignored member of the family. After all, it tells you nothing that you can't see separately in the 100 and 250 versions.

The FTSE 100, 250 and 350 all contain precisely the number of companies that are in their names but the other indexes that are worth looking at are elastic. They grow or shrink according to the number of companies that happen to be kicking around.

FTSE Small Cap index and FTSE Fledgling index

The FTSE Small Cap index covers the smaller (but not quite the smallest) companies with a stock market listing. The smallest of all go into the FTSE Fledgling index.

FTSE All-Share

Just to show that we have one big happy Footsie family, all the companies included in the various indices are lumped together in the FTSE All-Share index, which gives us an overall view of the main stock market board.

The Footsie family has a cousin, the AIM index, which, as its name implies, comprises the stocks quoted on the Alternative Investment Market.

There are also FTSE indices for the different sectors such as banking, construction, mining and leisure. These enable investors to gauge how well a particular company is faring compared with its *peers*, as its rivals are referred to.

Weightings

Every day some shares go up, some go down and some are unchanged. That happens even when the stock market as a whole is moving strongly in one direction or another. In addition, some shares may move heavily on a particular day while others change just one or two pence.

Each index must therefore calculate the average overall movement of the constituent companies. Companies are weighted according to their stock market capitalisations so share price movements of larger companies have a greater impact than those of smaller companies.

This prevents a sharp change in the share price of a small company having a disproportionate effect on an index.

Figures given on the FTSE website (www.ftse.com) show that on 31 March 2007 oil giant BP was the largest company in the country with a market capitalisation of just over £107bn. It accounted for 7% of the FTSE 100 calculation and 5.7% of the All-Share index.

Pharmaceuticals group GlaxoSmithKline had a market cap of £80.5bn so its weighting of 5.26% of the FTSE 100 index was roughly double that of its rival Astrazeneca, whose market cap of £42bn was allocated a weighting of 2.7%.

COMPANIES C

11.

Company Focus

What does the company do?

Companies and groups

Just as stocks and shares have become synonymous, so too the terms *company* and *group* have become interchangeable.

Strictly speaking, a company is one single business entity while a group is a group of companies all under the same ownership.

In a group, there will be a *parent* company that owns the various parts of the empire, which are the *subsidiary* companies kept separate for administrative convenience because they are into different lines of business or they operate in different countries.

Sometimes the parent company produces goods and services as well. In some cases the parent company does little itself and simply exists as the umbrella under which the subsidiaries operate. In that case the parent is a *holding company* and the subsidiaries are *operating companies.*

A company concentrating on just one line of products or services may not need to split itself into different units but if it does do so it will form *divisions* with the head of each division reporting to the one chief executive.

Dividing groups or companies in this way means it is easier to see which part of the operations are doing well and to spot problems as they arise.

What a company does

You need to have a good idea of what a company actually does before you invest in it. You wouldn't buy a tin off the supermarket shelf without knowing what was inside it, would you?

Some companies compete head on with others producing the same range of products or services; others try to find a niche market, concentrating on just one product where they are the biggest or only player.

Some companies believe in having a wide spread of products so that if demand falls off for one they have other lines to fall back on; while some specialise so they know their business inside out (a tactic referred to as *sticking to their knitting*).

Some concentrate on the UK, or even just one region; others want to go out and conquer the world.

Assessing a company

How to assess a company

Having established what the company does, you should consider whether it is expanding. Are sales rising or falling? While turnover is less important than profits, a company that is selling less and less is not going to survive long unless it can stabilise its income.

Is the company a heavy user of energy or fuel? It is likely to be suffering from higher costs unless it is able to pass those costs on in increased prices to its own customers.

Another important consideration is the extent to which the company has fixed costs such as offices and factory production lines. If sales go up and costs remain fairly static then profits will automatically rise. However, if sales fall and costs cannot be cut, the effect on profits can be pretty dramatic.

The importance of management

No one tactic guarantees success or is doomed to failure. You are looking for companies that demonstrate that they know what they are doing, whatever it is. Good management counts for a great deal.

So you want to know if top executives have changed recently. A poorly performing company can be turned round by new management who have fresh ideas and are determined to prove a point. A great company can tail off when the driving forces retire.

Really well-run companies plan for the succession. They avoid having the two top men, the chairman and the chief executive, retire at the same time. They set the search for a successor rolling in good time. Finding a high quality candidate for a top job can take months of searching by expensive recruitment firms popularly known as *headhunters*.

So management matters. But so does what the company does. Some sectors such as construction and housebuilding have been expanding for years despite interest rate rises while shops have struggled to cope with intense competition in the high street and with the incursions of online retailers.

Where to find information on a company

Ascertaining this information may seem daunting but you should try to build up as accurate a picture of a prospective investment as you can before committing your cash and it is not as difficult as you think.

Listed companies maintain websites with up-to-date information on what the company does, its financial performance, who the directors are and a host of other facts. From August 2007 AIM companies have been obliged to maintain a website with key information. Get Googling!

The website will also contain press releases and any trading statements the company has issued and copies of the annual report and the most recent company results. These give you a picture of how the directors assess the company's performance over the past year and the outlook for the coming months.

Do read any such pronouncements with a critical eye, though. The directors may be putting the best gloss on a difficult situation. If they have delivered on promises in the past they are more likely to do so in the future. Repeated broken promises are a warning sign and you should be loath to take mere platitudes at face value.

It is true that past performance is no guarantee that there will be more of the same in the future. However, past performance is the most accurate guide you have got.

Which companies to invest in

Do not invest in companies you do not understand. For example, if a company develops drugs and you cannot grasp the intricacies of Phase I, II and III trials – not many people do – then avoid the sector until you do. If you want to invest in insurance brokers and reinsurance companies, you had better find out what Lloyd's of London is all about.

Nor should you go to the other extreme and invest only in the sector you happen to work in on the grounds that that is all you understand. Portfolios should be balanced with one stock in each of a range of say ten sectors to give you a fair cross section. If you bought shares in HSBC, Royal Bank of Scotland, Barclays, Lloyds TSB and HBoS and nothing else you would be up the creek if banking shares went into a dive. Don't believe it can't happen. It can, even to banks.

The notion of investing only in ethical companies has become trendy in recent years. By all means follow your conscience but bear in mind there is hardly any company in existence that you can't find some objection to. Placing any kind of restriction on which shares you buy can limit your opportunity to make money. You can make only ethical investments and succeed; it is just more difficult.

12.

Profit And Loss

Companies publish their accounts twice a year:

1. the ones issued after the end of the half year are the *interims*, and

2. those issued after the full year are called the *prelims*.

Strictly speaking the accounts are issued in the annual report but a full, preliminary version covering the 12 months is issued through the stock exchange so you do not have to wait longer than necessary. Hence the term 'prelims'. Rest assured, these are the real accounts.

You don't have to understand every detail in a company's accounts but you really should not contemplate making an investment without some basic idea of how well the company is doing.

Unfortunately attempts over the years to improve accounting standards have made company accounts more opaque rather than easier to understand so we shall look at the important elements that give you a clear picture of what is going on.

There are two parts to the accounts:

1. **profit and loss account**, which tells you what went on over the past six or 12 months: how much money came in, how much was spent, how much tax is due and what dividend is proposed, and

2. **balance sheet**, which tells you the state of play at the end of the period, effectively how much the business was worth at that moment in time.

In this chapter we will look at the first part, the profit and loss account, the next chapter will deal with the balance sheet.

Analysis of a sample company accounts

For their commendable simplicity and clarity, we show in our table the annual results as issued by a software company called EG Solutions on 22 March 2007.

Figure 1: sample company annual results

Profit and Loss Account for the year ended 31 January 2007

	Year ended 31 January 2007 £'000	Year ended 31 January 2006 £'000
Turnover	5,472	5,879
Cost of sales	(1,710)	(1,572)
Gross profit	3,762	4,307
Administrative expenses	(4,164)	(3,569)
Operating (Loss)/profit	(402)	738
Other interest receivable	113	50
Interest payable	–	(19)
(Loss)/Profit on ordinary activities before tax	(289)	769
Tax on profits	116	(239)
(Loss)/Profit for the financial year	(173)	530
Earnings per share - basic	(1.3p)	4.4p
- fully diluted	(1.3p)	4.3p

Let's take it from the top.

Turnover

Turnover – which is increasingly referred to as *revenue* these days – is the total amount of money that EG received for its products over the 12 months. We can see by looking at the columns that turnover fell slightly compared with the previous year. This is not a good sign as you should prefer companies with rising sales but it is not a disaster provided there is a reasonable explanation.

Cost of sales

Cost of sales represents the raw materials and labour that went into the product. Note that this figure appears in brackets as it is a negative figure;

it is money going out of the company. These costs are deducted from turnover to give *gross profits*.

Gross profit

If the company is recording a loss at this stage it has serious problems and you will need a pretty good explanation to even think about buying the shares. A gross loss would mean that it costs more to produce the goods than the price at which they can be sold, hardly an encouraging sign.

Administrative expenses

Companies have other expenses that are not directly connected to the product itself. Examples are wages of administrative and marketing staff. These are described in this statement as *administrative expenses*; in other cases they may be called *overheads* or *central costs*.

There are some grey areas as to which category an expense should go into, for example electricity and storage, but don't worry about that as long as the company is using the same definitions each year so you can make fair comparisons. The important thing is to check whether sales are going up faster than costs (good news) or whether costs are going up faster than sales (bad news).

In this particularly case, costs were rising faster than sales. The reason, as explained in an accompanying statement, was that the company had expanded in anticipation of higher sales which were unfortunately delayed.

Operating profit or loss

After deducting administrative expenses, which appear in brackets as it is money going out, we arrive at the *operating profit or loss*. We can see that in the year to January 2006, EG made a profit of £738,000 while a loss of £402,000 was incurred at the operating level in the year to January 2007. The loss appears in brackets to indicate that it is a deficit.

The operating profit or loss represents the financial performance of the actual business. The company then calculates the interest it paid on any money borrowed or any income it received from cash in hand.

In the year to January 2006, EG had a cash surplus for part of the year and earned £50,000 on it. But it also paid out £19,000 on borrowings, a figure that appears in brackets because it is an outgoing. In the following year there were no bank borrowings but £113,000 was earned in interest.

Pre-tax profit or loss

After interest is accounted for we reach the *pre-tax profit or loss*. This is arguably the most important line in the profit and loss account. In the final reckoning, it shows whether the company has come out ahead. If this line in the accounts shows consistent improvement it doesn't really matter too much what is happening higher up. Your dividends will be paid out of the profits and if the profits go up then so, over time, will the share price.

Alas, the taxman will also want his cut. He took £239,000 out of the profits in the first year, a figure that goes in brackets because it is cash going out of the company. In the second year, when a pre-tax loss was recorded, a tax refund of £116,000 eased the pain. This figure is shown without brackets because it is a credit.

Profit or loss after tax

That leaves us with the profit or loss after tax, also referred to as the *post tax* figure. As always, a loss is shown in brackets.

Earnings per share

You will notice that EG has kindly added a line showing earnings per share. This is very important to you. It is calculated by dividing the profits after tax by the number of shares in issue and shows the amount of profit for each share that you hold.

You may find two EPS figures in some accounts, one *diluted* and one *undiluted*. The undiluted figure is the real figure; the diluted figure is what EPS would have been if any convertible shares had been converted into ordinary shares or if any outstanding share options had been exercised.

As we noted right at the start of this book, all ordinary shares have an equal stake in the company. When new shares are issued, your holding stays the same but there are now more shares in existence so the company is divided up into more slices. You will hold a fractionally lower percentage of the company. This effect is referred to as *dilution*.

The earnings per share figure is particularly important if the company has made an acquisition that was paid for in shares. Any extra profits from the acquisition as well as those from the existing business now have to be divided up among more shares.

Dividends

Dividends are paid out of earnings. If a company makes earnings of 10p per share and pays total dividends (the interim plus the final dividend) of 5p then you know there is easily enough cash to pay the dividends.

This calculation is known as *dividend cover* – a reference to how comfortable you can feel about the dividend. As far as one can set a norm, companies aim to cover the dividend roughly twice, in other words earnings per share are double the total dividend payment. This allows some leeway to maintain the dividend at the same rate next year even if the company does not do quite as well.

It also means that the company has a surplus that can be used as *working capital*, to expand the business, to buy new machinery, to acquire another company or to repay bank borrowings.

As long as the dividend is covered by earnings at least once, then profits are sufficient to pay the dividend. However, if cover falls below one then the company will have to draw on its reserves to pay part of the dividend. The reserves are the cash that was tucked away from profits in previous years when the dividend was covered more than once.

If the company makes a loss per share, then the entire dividend will have to be paid out of reserves. This is clearly a worrying sign unless there are genuine hopes that the company will return to making a profit soon.

Companies cannot go on drawing down reserves indefinitely. Indeed, when the reserves are used up it is illegal to pay a dividend.

These are the main lines that you definitely need to know in reading a profit and loss account but you will see other entries which can vary from company to company.

Exceptionals and extraordinaries

Particularly contentious in the profit and loss account are *exceptional* and *extraordinary* items. Companies will attempt to pick out large one-off items and list them separately on the grounds that they distort the *underlying* figures. By underlying we mean the normal business profits that allow us to make meaningful comparisons from year to year.

One-off items would include the sale of a property that was no longer needed. Say a company had two factories making the same item. Putting the whole production into one factory might be more efficient and it would then be possible to sell the empty factory and put the proceeds to good use.

That would create an extraordinary profit from the sale of the factory ("extraordinary" because the main activity of the company was not investing in property – and such profit would be unlikely to recur the following year). On the other hand, deciding that assets previously regarded as valuable were after all worthless would create an extraordinary loss.

No-one has come up with a satisfactory definition of what constitutes an extraordinary item and what makes an exceptional item.

One definition is that–

- an **extraordinary item** is an abnormality that arises from events or transactions that fall outside the ordinary activities of the business and are therefore not likely to recur;

- an **exceptional item** is an unusual large item that falls within the normal activities of the company.

Case study: Taylor Woodrow

Taylor Woodrow builds houses in the UK and the US. While the British housing market remained buoyant, many states in the US saw a severe fall in house sales after successive rises in interest rates left mortgage payers badly overstretched.

Housebuilders tend to own enough land to build on for four or five years and Taylor Woodrow owned land in the US and had options to buy more land to meet its future needs. Payments had been made to acquire this land, which was valued in the company's accounts accordingly.

In 2006 Taylor Woodrow decided that its US land was worth £21m less than it had previously reckoned, so an asset write-off of £21m appeared in the accounts for that year.

Unfortunately the housing situation became worse in Florida and California, two states where Taylor Woodrow had large house building projects, and a further £25m was written off land values in May 2007.

None of this actually cost Taylor Woodrow any cash at the time of the write-offs. The land and options to buy land had already been paid for. However, the reduction of the value of these assets had to be recorded in the profit and loss account as an extraordinary loss.

If you think that this is all rather imprecise you are in good company. Some analysts argue that there is no such thing as either and that all profits and losses should be lumped together.

Certainly it is true that many so-called extraordinary losses are really normal business costs that would usually have been spread over several years. In any case, as far as the investors are concerned a profit is a profit and a loss is a loss. After all, routine sales made this year might not be repeated in the future. Is a big contract win an extraordinary item? Surely not, but it could seriously affect profits from one year to the next.

Extraordinary and exceptional items must always be explained in the results statement. Usually there will be a separate column next to the table of results directing your attention to relevant notes right at the end of the statement, way after the balance sheet and any other tables such as cash flow that the company might care to include.

If in doubt, go by the pre-tax profit or loss, bearing in mind any items that may have caused a distortion. A loss, extraordinary or otherwise, means the company is less able to increase its dividend while a whacking great extraordinary gain can bring a special, extra dividend.

What you are looking for is whether the company is on an improving trend. If the profit figures are, on the whole, moving upwards (or the loss downwards) then you will naturally be reassured. Always, though, retain at least a grain of suspicion. If you are doubtful about what a company's profit and loss account is saying, there are plenty more companies about and you can't invest in all of them.

Cash flow

There may be a line in the accounts showing whether cash has flowed in or out of the company. Cash flow is not the same as profit. For instance, a company may invest heavily in new machinery. This will take cash out of the business in the current year, while depreciation of the asset will be taken out of profits bit by bit over several years.

Cash flow is likely to be more lumpy than profits so don't be too worried if some years cash flows out and other years it flows in. You should only be concerned if cash flows out constantly.

EBITDA

You will occasionally see a line in the results showing *EBITDA* or possibly *EBIT*. This was a device used in the dotcom boom to make unprofitable companies look profitable, or at least minimise the losses.

EBITDA became highly discredited when loss making dotcom companies ran out of money and crashed but it still persists and you should be extremely suspicious if you see a company pushing the EBITDA figure rather than the pre-tax profit figure. It almost certainly means that the company is making a pre-tax loss.

EBITDA stands for earnings before interest, tax, depreciation and amortisation. It is roughly equivalent to operating profit except that it may be shown as earnings per share rather than a total figure, in other words the profit has been divided by the number of shares in issue.

As you can see, it is calculated before a number of deductions, which is why the figure tends to be flattering and hence beloved by companies losing money. The case for ignoring these deductions varies from weak to non-existent.

Let us take the items one by one as they appear in this ludicrous acronym.

Interest

Interest we all understand. The company borrows from the bank and it has to pay interest on the debt, as we all do. If a company borrows heavily to finance its operations, then those operations must produce enough income to cover the interest bill, otherwise there's not much point in bothering to get out of bed in the morning.

Now companies can, for a limited period, run up debt without repaying it and even without paying all the interest as it is incurred, just as you can run up bills on your credit card and get away with simply coughing up the minimum amount. This state of affairs can not, however, go on indefinitely.

Interest payments are a genuine part of business expenses and *cannot* be ignored in calculating profits.

Depreciation

Taking depreciation out of the equation is slightly, just slightly, more acceptable. Where a company buys capital equipment, say a piece of machinery, it will last for several years. Once it is paid for, there is no need to splash out on a replacement until it wears out.

Nonetheless, it is prudent to write off a percentage of the value of the equipment year by year. This is rather like the value of your car. You pay £10,000 because that is what it is worth new but after just one year it will have lost about a quarter of its value to around £7,500 and after three years it will probably be worth less than half what you paid for it.

Companies therefore depreciate assets to represent dwindling values. Failure to include depreciation in the profit figure would mean taking a great chunk out of profits in a single year when the equipment needed replacing.

Interest and depreciation, therefore, are genuine expenses and should definitely be included when calculating profits.

Amortisation

Omitting *amortisation* is more reasonable. Amortisation occurs when a company buys another company. Say the acquisition has assets of £100m but it is a good little earner and it is bought for £120m because of its potential. The extra £20m is referred to as goodwill. This will be written off in the annual results in equal amounts until all the goodwill is accounted for, a process known as amortisation.

This is arguably an accounting technicality rather than a normal business cost.

Tax

Finally we come to T for tax. This is certainly fair enough. All companies produce figures for pre-tax and post tax profits. However, we do need to be sure that the company can afford to pay its tax bill at the end of the day and you don't know that from the EBITDA figure.

In May 2001 the management of Colt Telecom reiterated its confidence that the company would meet expectations for full year EBITDA of £40m-£50m. An investment journal commented at the time: "This will provide investors with some reassurance that Colt is not suffering from economic slowdown"; and to add to the cheer a major broker rated Colt Telecom shares a buy. Over the following 12 months the shares fell 96%.

Therefore be highly suspicious of EBITDA. It does not give a true picture of how the company is doing.

Seasonal sales

Some companies make most of their money in one particular part of the year or around a specific date. Such companies with seasonal sales and profits will tend to put the worst part of the year into the first half so they can always hold out the hope of better things to come if early sales slump.

Many obvious examples spring to mind.

Despite the popularity of winter sports among those who can keep their balance on the piste, holiday companies sell the overwhelming majority of their deals for the summer season. It is hard to think of a holiday provider that does not make a loss every winter.

Jewellers, on the other hand, make most of their money in December as conscience-stricken husbands attempt to make up for the past year's indiscretions.

Chocolates also sell heavily at Christmas but they have a bonus at Valentine's Day and at Easter. Spring is a time when a young man's fancy turns not only to love...but also to garden centres.

Do not, however, rush out to buy shares in Thornton's at the beginning of February just because sales are about to take off for a couple of weeks.

The peaks and troughs of the sales seasons are *factored in*, that is taken into account, when investors assess the shares. They will shoot up or down only if the company subsequently reports a particularly good or poor peak season compared to the same period the previous year.

Companies with seasonal sales need a good supply of cash or available bank loans handy to see them through the thin months so by all means check that sufficient finance is available. By placing their year end just after the busiest period they ensure that debt levels are at their lowest or cash in hand at its highest when the figures are produced.

Segments

The company may break its turnover and profits down into segments so you have a better idea of seeing which bits are doing well and which are causing problems.

A housebuilder such as Barrett Developments, with sites all over the country, may split its report into regions. This is important if, for instance, house prices in the south east are taking off while those in Yorkshire are marking time. You can see whether the company is more heavily committed to the thriving parts of the country or the less well favoured.

An international company such as Imperial Tobacco will tell you how its sales are going in various parts of the world. This can be important because the West has been running a long campaign to alert smokers to health risks while Third World countries are a growing market. Shareholders want to know if sales are being pushed in the fastest expanding market.

There is no rule that says how companies should divide up their regions – indeed there is no obligation to divide the results up at all. Much will depend on how widely the company is committed geographically.

Wolseley, the building products supplier, divides in two between Europe and North America. Others may split Europe into north and south or east and west. Some companies with small operations in Africa may have an EMEA region – Europe, the Middle East and Africa. Sometimes Asia Pacific lumps the Far East and Australia/New Zealand together.

An alternative to dividing into geographic areas is to split the business into products or services.

For example, John Menzies, better known as a distributor of newspapers and magazines to newsagents and supermarkets around the UK, has branched out into the somewhat unrelated world of ground handling services at airports.

Don't laugh…the news distribution is shrinking along with newspaper circulations while moving air passengers and cargo is rapidly becoming the larger part of the business. Splitting the results into these two segments gives a clearer picture of the group.

Don't worry too much about how a company *segmentalises*. In the end it is the total for the company that matters. Breaking down the figures is just an extra help for you in analysing and assessing the company as a potential investment.

Comparing like with like

It is important in judging whether a company's performance is improving to know that the latest figures are genuinely comparable with the previous year. Fortunately companies go to much greater pains these days to ensure that they are, even producing a second set of figures to eliminate distortions.

Companies may produce accounts for *continuing businesses* which strip out the contributions from operations that have been sold during the year.

Retailers in particular will produce figures for total sales and also for *like-for-like sales*. Total sales will include sales made at stores opened in the course of the year; like-for-likes tell you what happened at stores that traded throughout the past two financial years to give a fair comparison.

The like-for-like figure gives you a genuine indication of whether sales are improving or if they are simply being boosted by the company opening new stores.

The audit

It is not necessary to have interim accounts audited but full-year results must be checked by an independent firm of auditors which will normally sign the accounts as a *going concern*. In essence that means the auditor is satisfied that the company is not about to go bust.

If the auditor has any reservations it will *qualify* the accounts. This is very unusual but can happen if the auditors are not satisfied that the company has enough cash to keep going, or the company and auditors disagree over the way figures should be presented.

There are three reasons why auditors may qualify a company's accounts:

1. They are unable to check some information.

2. They disagree with the way that an item has been treated in the accounts.

3. They feel that the accounts do not give a true and fair view of the company's financial position.

Case study: Jarvis

One high profile case of auditors raising objections to a set of accounts was Jarvis, which provides support services such as maintaining rail track and schools. Much of the work was in the public sector, where work was allocated to private companies submitting the lowest tender.

However, Jarvis ran into difficulties during 2003, when some local authorities complained about the standard of work and some projects ran over budget. There were reports of delays in paying sub-contractors. The company was at this stage still under a cloud following the Potters Bar rail crash in May 2002 on a stretch of track that it maintained.

In the financial year to 31 March, 2004, Jarvis reported a loss of £246.7m, including extraordinary charges of £186.3m.

When these figures were released on 30 July, 2004, Jarvis admitted that the auditors were still going through the books and had raised three objections:

1. Doubts over whether Jarvis was still a *going concern*, in other words did it have enough cash to continue.

2. Whether Jarvis could recover money that it claimed was owing to it.

3. Whether future losses in construction contracts had been underestimated.

The auditors argued that some income recorded in the 2003-4 accounts would actually be received in the following financial year and it was prudent to include it in the 2004-5 figures instead.

Jarvis bowed to the auditors' wishes and within a month it produced new figures showing the 2003-4 loss to be £9m higher.

However, the auditors still put a note on the accounts expressing their doubts over whether Jarvis was a going concern, even though the group's lenders put up £25m of additional banking facilities and promised to continue their support through to the following March. Jarvis was forced to set about a drastic reorganisation that included selling parts of the business.

Shareholders did well to heed this warning and get out. In November 2004 Jarvis admitted that it was using cash from disposals to keep going rather than to reduce debt. Just before Christmas it warned that it had only enough money to last for another month.

Jarvis staggered on but in September 2005 shareholders were virtually wiped out. Those with fewer than 400 shares lost everything. Larger shareholders ended up with less than 5% of the company while ownership of the other 95% was handed over to the banks.

The repercussions have continued. Jarvis made a loss in the financial years to March 2005, 2006 and 2007. Some businesses and property have been sold and more shares have been issued to bring in cash. In June 2007 Jarvis was still unburdening itself of loss-making schools maintenance contracts.

13.

Balance Sheet

The balance sheet is an assessment of the assets and liabilities of the company at the moment the financial year ends.

* *Assets* are the things of value that the company owns including cash, property and machinery, while

* *liabilities* are what the company owes such as bills from suppliers.

The balance sheet will show the figures for the latest year end in one column and those for the previous year end in a separate column so you can see what changes in assets and liabilities have been incurred over the financial year.

As with the profit and loss account, items on the balance sheet can vary from company to company and you do not need to understand every single line comprehensively but it is useful to get the general picture so that you can assess the overall health of the company and whether it is moving in the right direction.

Also note that, once again, assets are shown as positive figures on the balance sheet while liabilities are shown in brackets.

Fixed assets

The first line on the balance sheet will normally be *fixed assets*. These are items such as machinery that are used by the business. They are fixed in the sense that they do not vary from day to day in the way that cash in hand or debts do. They are calculated on the basis of what they cost in the first place minus an amount written off the value to cover depreciation or, in the case of property, they are revalued by an independent surveyor at set periods.

This figure may be subdivided into:

- *tangible assets*, which are things you can see and touch such as equipment and property, and

- *intangibles* such as goodwill that is a vaguer valuation.

Current assets

Then come *current assets*. These may be subdivided into cash at bank and debts that are owed to the company and are due to be paid within 12 months. In other words, these are assets that the company could reasonably hope to lay its hands on fairly quickly.

Current liabilities

After that we have *current liabilities*, the amounts that the company is due to pay to people such as its suppliers within the next 12 months.

You deduct current liabilities from current assets. If the figure is a positive one, that figure is called *net current assets*; if you end up with a negative figure the company has *net current liabilities*.

The point of this little sum is to see whether the company faces a potential outflow of funds over the next 12 months or whether it has a buffer.

Apart from current liabilities there may be long term liabilities such as a loan that is not due to be repaid within 12 months. As an alternative to issuing shares, companies may raise money through *bonds*, which are loans raised from investors rather than banks. They are often referred to as *loan stock*.

Net assets

When you deduct total liabilities from total assets you end up with *net assets*, which again is usually a positive figure but in the case of a company in financial difficulties could be a negative figure (that is, the liabilities exceed the assets) and this will be shown in brackets.

We mentioned that balance sheets can vary according to what line of business the company is in. For example, a bank's balance sheet is likely to contain several more lines covering items such as customers' deposits, financial derivatives and the like. The important lines remain, however, total assets, total liabilities and net assets.

Finally we come to capital and reserves.

Capital reserves

First we have the *called up share capital*, which is the number of shares that have been issued multiplied by the nominal value of the shares. So if a company issues 100m shares with a nominal value of 50p each then the called up share capital will be £50m.

As we noted in the sections on rights issues and share placings, shares may be issued for more than their face value. The extra amount goes into what is called the *share premium account*, which is usually shown on the balance sheet.

The balance sheet will also show *reserves*. These are profits built up over the years and may include property revaluations. It is from these reserves that dividends are paid.

Where a company has made more losses than profits over the years there will be a *retained loss* which is the accumulated deficit. A company with a retained loss cannot legally pay a dividend until that loss is wiped out. This stops companies from paying dividends with money it does not have.

14.

Potential Nasties

There are danger signs to watch for in trading statements which may be issued separately or alongside a company's results.

If you are superstitious and believe that bad news always comes in threes then you will feel at home with profit warnings. When things go wrong, it is rare for them to be sorted out at one go. Three profit warnings is the norm, though there can be many more.

Case study: HMV

Figure 2: share price of HMV, 2005-2007

The events at HMV over a period of nearly two years demonstrate how bad news rarely comes in single doses and how the occasional slowness of the market to react can present opportunities for alert investors to cut and run.

HMV, which owns the Waterstone's bookshops as well as the HMV music stores, is a well known name on the high street, which may account for why the stock market was reluctant to recognise the scale of the problems.

The first warning signs came in June 2005 when HMV reported like-for-like sales down 1% in the latest seven weeks. The shares were around 230p at that stage but they continued rising to the top side of 250p despite growing signs that supermarkets and online retailers were muscling into HMV's territory with lower prices.

There was no hiding from the AGM statement in the following September, though. By then total sales in the UK and Ireland had fallen 3.7% compared with the same period of the previous year, including like-for-like sales down by an alarming 9.2%.

The shares plunged below 200p.

Undeterred, HMV management blithely launched into a bid for Ottakar's, a book chain that was suffering from the same problems as Waterstone's, and was prepared to pay a very generous 440p a share for the privilege.

This unfortunate distraction was cut short by the launch of an inquiry by the Competition Commission, which was worried that two large book chains would no longer be competing with each other. Thus the distraction continued for months as HMV awaited the outcome of the inquiry.

There was plenty within their own business for HMVs directors to worry about. In January 2006 they admitted: 'The competitive pressures faced by our UK businesses made trading very difficult during the autumn period.'

This admission, together with news that sales in the UK and Ireland had fallen further over Christmas, sent the shares sharply lower again. It was only expansion in newer markets in Canada and Asia that was keeping sales going.

Shareholders found immediate relief when investment company Permira expressed an interest in bidding for HMV. The bounce in the shares at this point presented an excellent opportunity for shareholders to get out but was yet another distraction for the HMV board.

Permira indicated that it was prepared to offer 190p a share and raised the stakes to 210p in March 2006, both figures being rejected as too low by the HMV board, which declined to even talk to Permira.

Instead HMV got embroiled once again in buying Ottakar's after clearance from the Competition Commission, paying just 285p a share for a company that only a few months earlier it thought was worth 440p.

This further distraction came as sales were falling 1.5%, including 5.7% like-for-like, in a trading statement in May, followed by sales down 2%, including 5.7% like-for-like, by July, when full year results showed profits down by a fifth.

Another sales decline was reported in September, a profit warning was issued in December, another sales decline came over Christmas and finally, in March 2007, a warning followed that trading conditions had deteriorated further as even the overseas operations were falling back.

It is true that this long litany of misfortunes came during a period of tough high street conditions, for which one might sympathise with the HMV management, but you don't invest on sympathy.

Throughout the downturn HMV attempted to put the best gloss it could on the situation, encouraging unsuspecting investors to stay in.

Lesson: always be on your guard.

In any case, HMV has added to its own troubles with strategy changes and store revamps that failed to deliver, by rejecting a takeover offer well above the subsequent share price level, and by buying a rival book store chain suffering from the same problems as its own outlets, thus compounding its difficulties.

Those investors who clung on to HMV shares despite all the warnings saw their holdings slide to 110p by the end of March 2007

Note that directors can be as reluctant as investors to face up to the fact that they got it wrong. Being human, they do not go out of their way to highlight the problems.

Case study: Uniq

Uniq, a supplier of chilled food, put out preliminary results covering the period to 31 December 2006. The statement, released on 26 March 2007, began thus:

Preliminary Results

Good progress made, recovery underway, debt eliminated and balance sheet strengthened

Key points include:

- Transformational highlights

- Completed the installation of strong leadership in each division

- Northern European restructuring plans in place

- Implementing restructuring plans in France and re-launching Marie

- Sold the Spreads and Belgian salads businesses for £288m

- Restructured balance sheet and eliminated debt

It all sounds very encouraging so far, yet the shares fell by 5.25p to 190.5p on the first stock market trade of the day and they stayed there, 2.7% down, for the rest of the morning.

Since Uniq had already fallen from a peak of 233.75p in early January, such a downbeat response seemed surprising, especially as the stock market generally was inching fractionally higher that morning.

When this happens, you need to dig deeper to find out what is really going on. Uniq's figures were rather messy that day, as the company had switched from a March year end to the calendar year, so the latest results covered only a nine-month period.

Uniq had in fact recorded a pre-tax loss from continuing businesses of £58.5m in the latest nine months, which is even worse than the £45.3m deficit in the previous 12-month period.

Those businesses that had been sold (see the fifth bullet point above) were the ones making the profits. Selling them off produced a short term gain, because Uniq was able to clear a loan negotiated the previous summer when the company had been struggling to keep going and had been forced to accept an onerous rate of interest when it went cap in hand to its bank.

The downside of these sales, though, was that profits would be harder to come by in the future, as was evident from figures for the remaining businesses. The UK operation, despite doing much better than it had done in 2005, had still run up an operating loss of £4m over the nine-month period; a sharp deterioration in Northern Europe meant a £5.4m loss there; and the previously profitable French businesses turned in a loss of £1.4m.

All this was in the statement. You just had to find it, as Uniq did not go out of its way to highlight the bad news, preferring to express its confidence in the future.

Banking covenants

When companies borrow money from the banks they give promises known as *covenants*. These will be along the lines of profits being sufficient to cover interest payments and assets being worth more than the loans secured against them.

You may have covenants on your house such as not being allowed to annoy the neighbours or park a caravan on the front lawn. The big difference is that while there is usually no-one to enforce housing covenants, the banks will certainly be keeping an eye on the ones that they impose.

Nor does a company find it any easier to wriggle out of its commitments than you do when you stray over your credit limit. Breaching banking covenants is *bad* news.

If the indiscretion is a minor one, or merely a technicality, the bank may decide to overlook it, especially if the company has kept the bank fully informed ahead of the actual breach.

At the other end of the scale, the bank may call in the loan and force the company into receivership. It will take such drastic action only in extreme cases. Banks, as you know, prefer to get their money back if they possibly can – and more besides.

So when a company goes along cap in hand the bank demands lengthy talks, for which it charges, and imposes higher interest rates. Thus the struggling company now finds it even harder to meet the bank's requirements.

It can take years of sound trading, and more expensive chats with the bank manager, to get out of this bind.

Kitchen sink accounting

You know the expression: everything but the kitchen sink? Struggling companies sometimes throw in the kitchen sink as well, usually when new management is installed to try to rescue an ailing business.

It doesn't mean that the company has branched out into plumbing. What happens is that all the bad news that can be dredged up is thrown into one set of very poor results in the hope that all the bad news can be got out of the way and things can only get better.

So assets are written down in value to zero, underperforming parts of the group are put up for sale and suddenly have no value, doubtful debts are declared uncollectible, stock is declared unsellable ... anything that can be counted as a loss is thrown in immediately.

This does mean a very poor set of results, probably with a horrendous pre-tax loss, but never mind because it can all be blamed on the old management.

The dividend, if there was one, is also scrapped but that too can be blamed on the outgoing directors.

Next year's results are almost certain to be better, since there are no more nasties to put in. Depreciation will be minimal since as much as possible was thrown into the kitchen sink job last time. If any of those doubtful bills get paid after all, that is a bonus. So even if the second year's results show another loss, as long as it is a smaller loss then the new management can claim that the worst is over (thanks to them, of course).

Strategic reviews

Companies are particularly keen on *strategic reviews*. They imply dynamic management seeking to take the business on to greater things and are always announced with a great fanfare.

Investors should not, however, get too carried away. Strategic reviews are popular with new chief executives and may have more to do with the new incumbent's desire to make a mark than to any need for change.

In these cases the review does give the new chief a chance to get to know the business rather than leap prematurely into changing the direction of the company and regretting the haste later.

The review allows fresh ideas to emerge and provides an opportunity for dead wood to be cleared out – just as long as it does not lead to change for the sake of it.

Of rather more concern is when the review indicates that something is seriously wrong with the business, which is why it needs looking at from top to bottom. In the worst case scenario, the review may be needed to avert the impending collapse of the business.

So if you see the announcement that a company has launched a strategic review, read on to find out what it is really all about. As you read, ask yourself why potential improvements to the business have not been spotted sooner.

Case study: Emap

Media company Emap publishes consumer and business magazines, arranges exhibitions and owns local radio stations. On 7 February 2007 it provided 'an update on the efficiency reviews we have been carrying out across our businesses and on trading'.

Emap had set out on not just one review but a whole series of them at the time of its interim results in November 2006, when revenue was down and profits were flat compared with the previous first half.

All was apparently going well with the reviews, which 'set out to transform how we operate, drive efficiencies and deliver real scale benefits'.

They reviews were 'close to conclusion' and there was an assurance that 'the plans we have developed will meet these objectives'.

There was little detail except that seven separate business-to-business magazine operations would be merged into one London property but Emap promised cost savings of £20m a year (at a cost of £30m plus capital investment of £10m, so it would take two years to recover the costs involved).

Then the statement turned to trading. Business-to-business operations were doing well but only because the figures had been boosted by acquisitions. Consumer media, particularly radio, had taken another turn for the worse.

As a result 'the outcome for the current financial year is likely to be toward the bottom end of market expectations'.

Emap shares fell from 808.5p to 774p that day, having been as low as 759p in the morning, and they continued to slide on worries over trading to close at 711p on 5 March 2007.

Pensions

Much has appeared in the press and on TV on the thorny subject of pensions and the potential black hole that they have created.

Briefly, there are two types of pensions:

1. defined benefits

2. defined contributions

These are described in more detail below.

1. Defined benefits

These pension schemes tell employees what benefits they will receive on retirement, typically a percentage of the employee's final salary, and were funded by contributions from employers and employees. The amount of money that needs to be available is determined by the commitment to pay pensions at a specified level.

It is hard to calculate how much money needs to be in the pot to meet pensions that will be paid many years in the future but while the stock market was booming in the 1980s and 1990s and pension funds were largely invested in shares, nobody much cared. Indeed, companies took pension 'holidays' during which they did not have to contribute to the funds.

After the stock market crash in 2000-3, many pension funds found themselves in deficit and the rules have been tightened to cover the worst case scenario. Companies have not only resumed contributions to these schemes, they have had to throw in extra dollops to fill the hole.

2. Defined contributions

In this type of pension the amount of money put into the pot by employer and employee determines the size of the pension at retirement age. This type of fund cannot be in deficit because the size of the pension is determined by the amount of money available, not the other way round as in the defined benefits scheme.

Naturally companies have been busy scrapping their defined benefits schemes and substituting with defined contributions schemes. In some cases existing employees are allowed to keep their perks and the new scheme applies only to new employees; in other cases even existing employees have been forced to switch.

These pension deficits are important to you as an investor for two main reasons. Where companies are saddled with a bill for filling up the hole, they will suffer from correspondingly reduced profits for several years until the hole is filled.

Companies do publish valuations of their pension fund assets and liabilities as calculated by specialists (known as actuaries) so you can see the size of any deficit. They will also report in their results how much extra they are putting in and how many years they expect to take to fill the hole.

The pension deficit can also be of crucial importance when a company attracts interest from a potential bidder. The trustees of the pension fund have a duty to ensure that anyone buying the company has also got the finances to make up any pension fund deficit.

This can be particularly important if the bid approach has come from a venture capital consortium because these are almost invariably loaded up with debt to pay for the proposed acquisition.

As an example, in March 2007 supermarket group Sainsbury was approached by a consortium of four venture capital companies while a second consortium of two US buyout funds was also attempting to put together the finance for a bid.

The trustees of Sainsbury's pension fund indicated that the shortfall in the fund was at least £477m; even after the supermarket chain made a large cash injection into the scheme in the previous year, and could be as high as £1bn. The deficit would continue to rise unless further contributions were made.

A similar situation arose when entrepreneur Philip Green, owner of the BHS stores, tried to launch a bid for Mark & Spencer two years earlier.

Pension fund trustees can in effect have the power to block takeovers as they carry out their duties to protect pension fund members.

This issue will gradually go away over time. The switch to defined contribution schemes will eliminate the danger of black holes in the future as the problem is effectively passed from the company to its employees, who simply get smaller pensions.

In addition, the extra contributions from the companies into existing defined benefit schemes, plus the rising values of investments, should eventually eliminate or at least alleviate the deficits.

INVESTING **D**

15.

Starting Out

First – study yourself

It can be a daunting prospect to invest in the stock market for the first time so it is very important to do your homework. Start by studying yourself.

Only you know what you can afford to invest, what risks you want to take or can afford to take, whether you want to invest for the short or long term and whether you want a steady stream of income to live on.

Before you invest, sit down with pen and paper and note your income and *all* your outgoings, including food, clothing, entertainment and holidays as well as any mortgage payments, utility bills and monthly instalments on furniture or electrical appliances.

You should consider owning your own home if you are renting. Like shares, property values can fall but they also rise over the long term and you have to live somewhere.

Most families these days own a car. If you do, you should allocate some cash towards the next one.

Indeed, you may feel more comfortable with some of your cash invested in *liquid assets*, that is money you can get hold of in an emergency at little or no notice such as savings in a building society account.

Shares are liquid in that they can be sold quickly in the stock market but there is always the danger that you find yourself having to sell just when the market is depressed. Keeping a pot of cash earning some interest but readily available gives you the leeway to hang on to shares that you believe will gain value and can then be sold at a higher price.

If you decide, despite reading this book, that you need the help of a financial adviser you must lay your soul bare. The adviser needs to know all your financial circumstances and your investment aims in order to give you the advice that suits you.

In the following chapters we will look at different investment strategies but first there are some general points worth noting.

Keep yourself informed

You don't have to sit at your computer screen watching share price movements all day. Leave that for the day traders, the people who make a living by buying in the morning and selling a few hours later.

You should, however, keep abreast of what is going on. Information is freely available in newspapers, specialist magazines and financial websites so there is no excuse for burying your head in the sand.

We noted in the section on companies that they are required to issue at least two announcements each year: the interim results and the full year results. These are usually accompanied by an indication of how trading is going.

In addition, companies have increasingly been issuing trading statements to mark the end of the half year and the full year.

In 2007, as part of the drive to ensure that companies keep shareholders fully informed, the European Union issued the Transparency Directive, so named because it is supposed to enable you to see right through the company.

UK companies with a full listing must now issue a trading update, called an *interim management statement*, after the first and third quarters of their financial years to supplement information issued alongside the half year and final results.

This ruling does not apply to companies with a quotation on AIM.

Factors that affect share prices

Share prices are on the move throughout the trading day. Those of the largest companies such as BP and Vodafone will change moment by moment as buying and selling ebbs and flows; those of the tiniest companies may move only sporadically and may go for several days without a change.

The main impetus for share price change is supply and demand. When buyers pile in, shares inevitably go up; a flood of sellers is bound to depress the market.

However, buying and selling pressure is the symptom rather than the cause. We need to look at why it is sometimes predominantly buyers and sometimes sellers who are out in force. We should note that on some days practically the whole market moves in one direction while at other times it is just particular sectors and sometimes just individual shares selectively.

Even when the market as a whole is moving in one direction, perhaps over a prolonged period, some shares will buck the trend. During the three year bear market in 2000-2003, when Footsie shares on average lost more than half their value, oil explorer Soco and financial broker ICAP both saw their shares increase by more than 400%.

Market movements

Reasons why the market as a whole moves

1. There is new UK economic news such as inflation figures.

2. Markets around the world are moving in a particular way and London joins the trend. Shares here are particularly influenced by large movements on the New York Stock Exchange as the US is the world's largest economy.

3. The market has moved strongly in one particular direction and investors take profits or look for bargains.

4. The world economy takes a turn for the better or worse.

Reasons why a sector moves

1. There is news specific to that sector, for instance a rise in oil prices will hit the shares of transport companies faced with higher fuel bills.

2. Sales of goods and services in one sector are affected by changes in consumer behaviour, such as the switch from high street shopping to buying on the internet.

3. Companies in a particular sector are expected to be involved in takeover activity.

Reasons why shares in a particular company move

1. Sales and profits are better or worse than expected.

2. The company announces that it expects to beat or fall short of analysts' expectations.

3. A rival company is winning its business or is struggling to keep its share of the market.

4. Rumours about the company circulate, particularly if the talk is of a takeover.

5. A takeover or an approach that could lead to a bid is announced.

6. There are changes to senior management.

7. Directors buy or sell shares in the company.

8. The board changes its strategy, perhaps deciding to seek new markets, expand overseas or sell loss making operations.

These are all logical reasons for share price movements, but it is also true that the stock market can, in the short term, be an irrational place and rises and falls sometimes seem to defy logic. Such movements are prompted by market *sentiment,* the general feeling in the market.

Shares may start to rise and punters leap onto the bandwagon for fear of missing an opportunity, only to fall off painfully when the bandwagon comes to an abrupt halt. Then shares may fall back sharply in what is known as a *correction*.

Interest rates

Why and how interest rates move

Interest rates used to be set by the Chancellor of the Exchequer and changes tended to come out of the blue. But one of the first things that Gordon Brown did when he moved into No. 11 Downing Street was to put the Bank of England in charge of interest rates.

The Bank has a Monetary Policy Committee (MPC) of nine men and women comprising the Governor of the Bank of England, the Deputy Governor, other senior Bank of England staff and outsiders appointed by the Chancellor. Its task is to keep inflation within prescribed limits, currently between 1% and 3% as measured by the Consumer Price Index.

Interest rates run in cycles, rising and falling over a period of months or years. Mercifully for investors the Bank tries to warn us of impending changes in interest rates and to give some idea of where we are in the cycle so there is no reason to get caught out.

The MPC meets early in each month and members vote on whether to raise rates, keep them as they are or reduce them. The majority vote prevails and if necessary the Governor has a casting vote. The decision is announced at noon on a Thursday.

Changes are normally a quarter point in either direction, although individual members have occasionally voted for half point changes. Minutes of the meeting, including voting figures, are issued later in the month. The Bank also issues a quarterly report so there are plenty of clues as to how the wind is blowing.

In broad terms, interest rates are raised when inflation rises above the 2% midpoint in the target range. Higher interest rates make debt more expensive, demand for goods is curtailed and consumers start to get twitchy. It becomes more attractive to save than to spend.

The effect of interest rates on share prices

Share prices are affected by changes in interest rates:

- **rising interest rates** are bad news and send share prices *lower*;

- **falling interest rates** are good news and send share prices *higher*.

Several reasons why higher interest rates are bad for shares are:

- If demand for goods and services falls (as consumers have less cash to spend), then companies will make reduced profits.

- The pound becomes more attractive for foreign investors to hold, so sterling rises on the foreign exchange market and British goods become more expensive abroad, so exports are affected.

- Companies that export from the UK or have operations abroad find that their profits are reduced when foreign currency is converted into more expensive pounds.

- Investors find it is more attractive to invest in bonds or even keep their cash on deposit because they are now being paid a higher rate of interest.

- Investors who take the risk of borrowing money to buy shares find it more expensive to do so.

- Preference shares fall in value because the fixed rate of interest becomes less attractive.

Rising interest rates are referred to as a *tightening of monetary policy*. When inflation falls the Bank of England can relax or ease monetary policy by cutting interest rates.

Now the factors we considered when discussing rising interest rates work in reverse. Consumers spend more and save less, which is generally good for the profits of UK companies. Bonds become less attractive, while borrowing money to buy shares offers a better hope of producing a decent profit.

Facing reality

The hardest thing for any investor to do is put hand on heart and admit: 'I got it wrong'. Even hardened professionals cling to shares as the price falls relentlessly in the vain belief that their precious investment must eventually prove justified.

None of us get it right all the time and sometimes you will have to bite the bullet and sell at a loss.

Some investors set a *stop loss*. They fix a price at 10% or 20% below the price at which they buy a particular share and resolve to sell if the share falls to that level. In that way any losses are limited.

There is no magic level at which you should set your stop loss. Set it too high and you will sell out before you have given the shares a real chance to perform. Set it too low and you risk a heavier fall if you really have picked a loser.

16.

Stockbrokers

You will need a stockbroker who is a member of the London Stock Exchange to carry out the transaction for you when you buy or sell shares. A broker is a go-between, in this case between you and the stock market.

Some large banks offer a dealing service to their customers so you can ask the bank where you have your current or savings account what facilities, if any, are available. The advantage is that you probably wander into your local branch from time to time to draw out cash or pay bills so you are likely to feel comfortable making an enquiry there.

You can buy with cash directly out of your account so there is no need to set up a new one.

The big drawback is that you may have to deal at *best price*, that is instruct the bank to buy or sell at whatever price it can get rather than have the flexibility to stipulate the price at which you are willing to deal.

The alternative, which need not be daunting, is to set up an account with a stockbroker. There is no shortage of them and wherever you live you should be able to find one in a town or city near your home, although in these days of mass communications this is not necessary.

Many people, though, do prefer to deal with an office that they can visit and meet a staff member to get a feel for the place and discuss their requirements. That way they will be a face, not just a name.

The London Stock Exchange website (www.londonstockexchange.com) has a full list of approved stockbrokers. Find 'Locate a Broker' in the Education section.

Or you can approach the Association of Private Client Investment Managers and Stockbrokers, an organisation that represents the overwhelming majority of brokers and investment advisers in Britain.

The APCIMS website (www.apcims.co.uk) not only has a list of stockbrokers but a search facility so you can narrow the list down to brokers in your area, those willing to handle your size of investment and the types of services you want.

You will be looking for a stockbroker who is happy to handle small clients, so don't start looking for the biggest names in the business. They probably won't want your account unless you are particularly wealthy.

If you are happy using the internet, there are online brokers. They tend to be geared to small accounts and they tend to be cheap.

Best of all is to find a friend or acquaintance who already has a stockbroker. If they are happy with the service they are getting, word of mouth counts for as much in this sphere as it does in finding a handyman or an electrician.

Decide how much you want to invest, either a lump sum or a regular investment, and tell the broker at the outset so you are quite sure they handle your size of account.

Some, but not all, brokers offer services such as self-invested pension plans (Sipps) and individual savings accounts (ISAs).

Now you must decide what kind of service you require.

Execution only

You take all the decisions. You decide what shares you want to buy or sell and your broker will quote the current price so you can decide whether to go ahead or not. When you buy shares you need to decide how much to invest in each company and calculate how many shares you will get for that amount of money.

If you are confident after reading this book, this is the service for you. You put in your order and the stockbroker buys or sells according to your instructions.

Advisory services

You still make your own decisions and the stockbroker will buy and sell only on your say-so but this time the stockbroker provides expert advice and guidance. Naturally you have to pay extra for the advice.

You should receive research notes produced by the brokers' analysts and advice tailored to your specific needs.

Charges vary from broker to broker so you will have to shop around. Given the vast number of stocks on the London Stock Exchange, you cannot expect your broker to cover every single one. Some brokers specialise in covering larger or smaller companies, others look at a fixed range of specific sectors. Always ask before you commit yourself.

Discretionary management

You hand over your cash and the stockbroker takes the decisions for you. You will need to make it clear what your investment objectives are, for example whether you want income or capital gains and whether you want to play as safe as possible or how much risk you are willing to take.

Confidentiality

Whichever service you decide to take, your stockbroker is under an obligation to keep your financial affairs confidential. This does mean that you can make a full and frank disclosure of your financial position without fear it will fall into the hands of the tabloid newspapers.

If you want advice from your stockbroker you must be completely open, otherwise the advice cannot be tailored to your requirements.

Costs

Commissions

The days of fixed commissions set by the London Stock Exchange have long since gone and brokers are free to set their own charges. Inevitably they will be restricted by the knowledge that rival brokers will undercut them if they charge too much.

The price of the service you select will vary from broker to broker, perhaps enormously.

Execution only is the cheapest, as you are doing all the real work. You will be charged so much per trade, either a fixed amount or a percentage of the value of the transaction. Expect to find that there is a minimum charge.

It can cost as little as £5 per trade and you might even get a special offer as a new customer.

Advisory services may levy a charge per trade, an annual fee or a mixture of both. Check how many analysts' notes you are entitled to per year.

For a discretionary service you will usually pay an annual fee, probably larger than for the advisory service as the broker is doing all the work. There could also be a charge per transaction so do give your broker clear instructions to avoid *churn*, making more buys and sells than necessary.

Your broker should not churn your account but if you feel that the number of deals being made are excessive, find another broker. The broker has discretion but not total control. You can stipulate, for example, that shares in a particular company must not be sold or that you do not want investments in companies you regard as unethical.

The broker should be prepared to set out the fees clearly and it is imperative that you ask what you are going to be charged. The money comes out of your investment pot.

Stamp duty

With all trades you will, unfortunately, have to pay stamp duty of 0.5% of the value of the transaction on all share purchases, though not on sales. Campaigns over many years to get this imposition removed have fallen on deaf ears. No wonder. The Chancellor of the Exchequer raises £3bn a year from stamp duty on share purchases.

Cold callers – a warning

You should deal only with reputable stockbrokers registered with the Financial Services Authority. In particular, you should be extremely suspicious of cold callers, the complete strangers who ring you on the telephone out of the blue.

The FSA has on its website (www.fsa.gov.uk) a list of known operators that are not kosher but the list is far from exhaustive. It cannot be, as dubious operations and outright crooks simply change their names once they are rumbled.

Although many pretend to be British operations with UK addresses, they are more likely to be working from Amsterdam or Barcelona and you will have no legal protection and no hope of compensation if you are fleeced. That UK address is probably a mailing address, not a real office.

Nor should you assume that a country such as Switzerland, with its reputation of strict financial rules, will look after your interests in preference to those of a Swiss national if push comes to shove.

The myriad ploys designed to part the gullible from their money are sufficiently numerous and fascinating to fill a book on their own but the general principle is that you are lumbered with an 'investment' that is unsellable, in sharp contrast to the London Stock Exchange which is all about creating a market for the mutual benefit of buyers and sellers alike.

A particular ploy is to offer shares in a company that is unquoted but which is supposedly coming to market soon. You are assured that the shares will soar when they are floated. It's all promises, most of them meaningless.

Ask yourself this: If something is too good to be true, why would you believe it?

17.

Fundamental Data

There are three ways of deciding which shares to invest in:

1. fundamental data

2. charting

3. gut feeling

The best policy may be to take a combination of the three and the more you invest the better your judgement will become. Fundamentals are based on hard facts about the company; charting follows movements in the company's share price; gut feeling is something that cannot be easily defined or taught.

If you get a feeling that a company is heading for trouble or is about to turn the corner, and you find that nine times out of ten you are right, by all means follow your heart. Otherwise it is probably best to stick with what is more tangible.

Fundamentals are the figures that the company puts out in its profit and loss account and in its balance sheet plus the calculations that you can make with those figures.

Through the fundamentals you can work out whether shares look good value.

Historic and prospective data

Figures published by the company cover periods of time that have elapsed. Their main advantage is that they are real figures. They tell you what really happened but they are historic. They do not in themselves tell you what will happen over the coming months.

Analysts employed by stockbrokers make forecasts covering up to 24 months ahead. These forecasts are referred to as *prospective* or *forward*. They have the big advantage of telling you what is likely to happen to revenue and profits so you can assess how share prices will be affected in the future. However, they are only forecasts, not actual figures, and they can be wrong.

Larger companies are researched by several analysts and it is possible to get a *consensus* or average view of expectations. Smaller companies may be researched by only one or two analysts, or there may be no forecasts at all.

There are two particularly important pieces of fundamental data that you should consider when deciding to buy a company's shares: *dividend yield* and the *price/earnings ratio*.

Dividend yield

The yield is particularly important if you are looking for steady income from your shares.

Do not assume that large dividends in terms of pence per share are necessarily more attractive. If the shares are more expensive then you need a bigger dividend to make the investment worthwhile.

Let us suppose that the shares in a company A cost you 100p and the company pays a dividend of 4p. For every £100 you put in, you get 100 shares and the dividend you receive will amount to £4. The yield is 4%, that is £4 on every £100 invested.

Shares in company B cost 200p each and the dividend is 5p. Although the dividend is 1p higher than at company A, the yield is only 2.5%. For every £100 you invest, you get only 50 shares so you receive only £2.50 in dividends. The yield is therefore 2.5%, of £2.50 for every £100 invested.

You can calculate the yield on any share quite simply by dividing the dividend by the price of the shares. Remember that *both* figures must be in pence (or, if appropriate, in euros or US dollars) so you are dividing like with like.

You can use the historic figure to get the *historic yield* or analysts' forecasts to calculate the *prospective yield*.

The following table gives examples of companies and their historic and forecast dividend yields (at the time of writing of this book).

Table 6: sample historic and forecast dividend yields

Company	Share price	Dividend(p)	Yield(%)	Projected Dividend(p)	Projected Yield(%)
United Utilities	634	44.9	7.1	46.0	7.3
Lloyds TSB Group	521	34.2	6.6	34.8	6.7
Rentokil Initial	158	7.4	4.7	7.4	4.7
Ladbrokes	366	13.2	3.6	14.2	3.9
Tesco	404	9.6	2.4	10.8	2.7
Capita Group	707	9.0	1.3	12.0	1.7
Antofagasta	608	4.2	0.7	13.7	2.3

The higher the yield, the greater your income for every pound invested. You may wonder why some companies have much higher or lower yields or dividends than average.

Companies look cheap when there are doubts about how well they will fare in the future while others look expensive because the market sees them as good investments that are highly likely to grow in value.

If there are reasonable hopes that the dividend will continue to rise for the foreseeable future, then investors may be happy with a low but solid yield. Where there are serious doubts about a company's profits and the possibility arises that the dividend will have to be cut in future, then investors will want a higher yield in the meantime.

Remember, the stock market is about risks and rewards. The greater the risk, the greater the reward you are entitled to expect if it all comes right in the end.

Price/earnings ratio

The second vital figure, particularly relevant to those looking for capital gains rather than income, is the price/earnings ratio, often referred to as the *rating* because it indicates whether the shares look cheap or expensive.

This ratio (usually abbreviated to PER or just PE) is calculated by dividing the price of the shares by the earnings per share after tax.

As with yield, you must divide pence by pence or euros by euros. But unlike the yield, where you get a better return from a higher figure, the price-earnings ratio identifies cheap shares as the ones with a lower figure. The lower the PE, the cheaper the share.

Also, as with the yield, a *historic PER* can be calculated from historic earnings per share, while a *forecast PER* can be calculated from forecast earnings per share.

The following table gives some examples of companies and their historic and forecast PERs (with figures accurate as of writing this book).

Table 7: sample historic and forecast PERs

Company	Share price(p)	EPS(p)	P/E	Projected EPS(p)	Projected P/E
ARM Holdings	147	3.1	47	5.1	29
ICAP	485	20.0	24	28.6	17
Unilever	1523	82.7	18	91.9	17
Barclays	640	53.2	12	73.2	9
Rolls-Royce Group	478	54.0	9	31.4	15
Legal & General Group	137	24.0	6	11.8	12

Generally, companies growing fast tend to have high PE ratios, while slow growth companies have low ratings. Certain industries (e.g. technology related) tend to be regarded as high growth and therefore attract high ratings; whereas other industries (e.g. utilities) are traditionally viewed as low growth and have low ratings. Companies in the same industry tend to have similar ratings. However, anomalies do occur and, as with the yield, a company's rating may look cheap for good reason. A lowly rating can indicate concern over the company's prospects, while a high rating reflects confidence.

18.

Charting

Chartists believe that shares gain a momentum that may or may not be justified by fundamental data.

We can see when a company is theoretically under or overvalued. The stock market can be particularly efficient at ironing out these kinks, so in theory a share price should not get far out of line before the laws of supply and demand pull it back into place.

However, the stock market can be an irrational place, running at least in part on what is referred to as *sentiment*, the overall feeling of investors towards particular shares or the market place in general.

If shares start to move in a particular direction, investors jump on the band wagon, sometimes in simple fear of missing out. The stampede can turn into a panic.

Chartists look for trends in the share price chart. They are right to say that once a share starts to move in a particular direction the trend often continues for much longer than investors expect. Private investors are particularly fond of grabbing profits too soon, selling out long before the share price rise is over, yet they cling to falling shares rather than admit they made a bad choice.

Charting is a highly specialised art and this book will deal only with the basics. Charting does not supply sure-fire tips for success, otherwise everyone would be doing it. Critics would say that, as with any other method of stock picking, the only certainty is that it tells you after the event what you should have done last week or last month.

The mantras of charting are that you go with the flow and the trend is your friend. As a general principle, chartists are willing to miss out on the early opportunities for buying on the cheap. They do not try to catch falling shares as they hit the bottom or to set the momentum going. They jump on the bandwagon once it is moving and enjoy the ride, hoping to get off just before it all comes to an end.

They look for those occasions when a share chart starts to draw a pretty picture and we will cover some of the key indications.

We can discuss here only the basics concept of charting. It is possible to write a whole book on the subject, or even on just one aspect of charting. People have done so.

Floors and ceilings

Chartists look for *support points*, a level in a particular share price where investors have in the past been tempted to buy, sending the shares higher. This is also known as a *floor*.

They are also wary of *resistance levels* or *ceilings,* points in the chart where shareholders have previously decided to take profits because they believed that the shares would not go any higher.

The chart of Go-Ahead, the bus and train operator, shows that 2,400p has been a crucial level for the shares.

Chart 6: Go-Ahead, examples of support and resistance levels

Early in 2007 the shares fell back each time they reached this level, as if they had hit a ceiling. Some investors felt that the shares had become overvalued around this level and they sold out at a profit.

Each time the shares rose back to 2,400p, investors who had previously bought at this level and seen the value of their holdings fall now had the opportunity to get out and some clearly did.

However, in late February and early March the shares twice broke strongly through the ceiling. Now 2,400p became a support level. Those who had sold at 2,400p in the false belief that the shares would fall, as they had done before, now saw the chance to get back in again.

The chart went on to set a new ceiling at 2,700p. Despite a sharp fall in the share price in early June 2007, the support level held at 2400p twice during that month.

Carpetright's share price shows how difficult it is to judge whether a ceiling has been broken decisively. On several occasions in 2006 and 2007 the shares seemed to have moved sharply higher through the ceiling just above 1,200p, only to fall back again.

Chart 7: Carpetright, examples of support and resistance levels

As a retailer of carpets, mats and vinyl flooring, Carpetright has been susceptible to interest rate rises because consumers became increasingly reluctant to commit themselves to more expensive purchases.

Another factor was at play. Speculation ebbed and flowed over whether Carpetright founder and chairman Lord Harris would make a takeover offer. Charts should always be read in conjunction with news flow.

Peaks and troughs

Shares do not run in straight lines up or down. Even on a good bull run there will be occasional small falls among the rises as some investors decide to take profits. Similarly, falling shares will perk up from time to time, as buyers provide support, before resuming their bear trend.

Case study: Morrison

Figure 3: share price of Morrison

Supermarket group William Morrison went through a difficult period after taking over the rival Safeway chain. Management simply lost control of the business. Sales at the Morrison stores suffered as attention was concentrated on converting the newly acquired stores to the Morrison format

That traumatic period was reflected in a bearish phase in the share chart lasting for two years from early 2004.

However, the problems were eventually resolved and Morrison shares set out on a steep bull run when, in the middle of 2006, they moved decisively above the downward sloping line linking the previous peaks.

When you see such a chart, draw a straight line joining as far as possible all the peaks and all the troughs. If each peak is higher than the previous peak, and if each trough is higher than the previous one, then the bull phase is still intact.

In the case of a rising share price, the troughs are more important than the peaks. The troughs mark the point at which buyers again outnumbered the sellers who were getting out, the point at which the shares found support. As long as the shares stay above the rising support line, they are still in a bull phase. When the share price drops below the line, it can be a signal to get out.

When shares are falling, with each peak below the previous peak and each trough below the previous trough, the shares are in a bear phase. This time the peaks are more important. They represent the falling level at which buyers lose enthusiasm and the sellers take over again.

If the shares rise above the line connecting the peaks, it is a signal that the bear phase could be over and it could be time to buy.

Note the words can and could. There is no guarantee that the trend is broken, just a strong indication. Share charts do not move in regular patterns so those straight lines cannot exactly touch every peak and trough spot on.

Rangebound

Figure 4: share price of Rentokil

Particularly where there is little change in a company's results over a period of time, shares may simply move sideways within a narrow range, waiting for that key item of news that will send them higher or lower. This time the line joining the peaks and the one joining the troughs are horizontal rather than sloping. Any breakout above the top line suggests that a bull phase may be beginning; a fall below the support line is a danger signal.

19.

Tips

Stockbroker analysts

Several stockbrokers employ analysts who pronounce on the merits or otherwise of companies with stock market quotations.

These analysts are required to pass examinations in order to register with the Financial Services Authority before they are allowed to make recommendations. The stockbrokers they work for will also be registered with the FSA and are required to ensure compliance with strict rules, particularly in terms of avoiding a conflict of interest.

Each analyst will cover a specific sector to build up expertise and each broker will cover a limited range of companies or sectors, or may specialise in covering just larger or only smaller companies. With nearly 2,000 companies quoted on the London Stock Exchange, including AIM companies, it would need quite an army to research and report on the lot.

Analysts do have access to directors of companies that they cover, especially when results are announced. Companies may hold analysts' briefings to answer questions arising from results or trading statements. They may take them on site visits; say to a manufacturing facility or a retail outlet.

However, companies are not allowed to pass sensitive information to analysts in private. Anything that might affect the share price must be put into the public domain.

Apart from their specialised knowledge and expertise in reading company accounts and balance sheets, analysts have more time than most private investors to study all the details and to offer a considered assessment. It is, after all, their job. They are, though, human and like all experts they can get it wrong.

Analysts draw up reports on the companies they cover, assess strengths and weaknesses and make forecasts of turnover and profits for the current financial year and the next one.

They will make recommendations on whether investors should buy or sell the shares. These reports are sent privately to the stockbroker's clients who have paid for the service. It is only fair that those who have paid up get first go at the assessment but a summary of the week's recommendations appears in various weekend newspapers as well as the *Investors Chronicle* and *Shares* magazine.

Interpretation of analysts' recommendations

The recommendations can be confusing because the terminology varies between brokers but generally they work on a scale from one to five, ranging from a confident buy recommendation, a less enthusiastic but still positive stance, a neutral position, a fairly negative position and a clear sell recommendation.

For clarity the table below sets out most of the different expressions used.

Table 8: terminology of analysts' recommendations

Hot	Lukewarm	Tepid	Chilly	Freezing
Strong buy	Buy	Hold	Sell	Strong sell
Buy	Add	Hold	Reduce	Sell
Buy	Overweight	Neutral	Underweight	Sell
Strong buy	Weak buy	Neutral	Weak sell	Strong sell
Buy	Outperform	Market performer	Underperform	Sell

You may wonder how it is possible to have different grades of buy or sell recommendations. Surely a buy is a buy and a sell is a sell?

Also confusing is that some analysts use 'buy' at the top end of the scale while others do not, and likewise they may or may not put 'sell' at the bottom of the scale. The lines can get a little blurred.

You would be quite right to raise such objections. Analysts, like the rest of us, can be mealy mouthed and hedge their bets. All you can assume is that analysts making a half hearted buy or sell recommendation feel less sure they are right than if they went the whole hog.

The implication with a *weak buy* is that you should buy some shares but not too many. With a *weak sell* you could sell some but not all of your holdings. This intention is more clear when *add* and *reduce* are used.

The terms *overweight* and *underweight* cause confusion. The analyst is suggesting that you should hold more or fewer shares in a particular company than you normally would. For example, if you tend to invest £2,000 in each company in your portfolio, overweight would imply buying say £2,500 worth while underweight would steer you to risking only £1,500.

Outperform, market performer and *underperform* are a bit of a cop-out. Instead of recommending whether you should buy or sell the shares, the analyst is assessing how they will fare in comparison with the rest of the stock market.

Supposing the market is steady, with little movement on the FTSE 100 or other indices. Then 'outperform' stocks will rise and 'underperform' stocks will fall if the analyst is right.

But if the stock market rises then even the 'underperform' stocks are likely to rise: they will just rise less than the rest of the market. In these circumstances an analyst can claim to have been right if an 'underperform' stock shows a modest rise.

Similarly if the stock market tumbles then even an outperforming stock can fall back.

As a general rule, treat 'outperform' as a buy indication and 'underperform' as a sell rating but view them with more caution than an outright recommendation.

Analysts may also advise investors to *avoid* a particular stock. Well, that at least is perfectly clear: don't buy the shares and if you already hold them sell them pronto. This is the strongest 'sell' recommendation of all, implying that you should not touch the shares with a bargepole.

Another recommendation occasionally seen is *take profits*, which is similar to 'sell' but with a subtle difference. A 'sell' recommendation implies that the company is doing badly; 'take profits' means that the shares have had a good run. The company is probably still in good shape; it is just that the shares have run up a little too quickly and might fall back to a more realistic level.

Finally we occasionally see shares labelled as *fair value* or *up with events*. This is an alternative version of 'hold' or neutral' and indicates that the market has got this one about right. In the view of the analysts there are no compelling reasons to buy or sell these shares.

Can analysts be trusted?

So, analysts are experts but can we trust them? After all, the stockbrokers they work for are touting for trade among the companies they write about. Surely they are under pressure to be nice, especially to companies that are employing their colleagues as advisers.

There has been heavy criticism in the past over the role of analysts. Stockbrokers were supposed to operate what were called *Chinese Walls* between different parts of their business, with analysts blissfully unaware which companies their colleagues were advising or buying shares in.

Imaginary walls as thick as the Great Wall of China would prevent information seeping through. This notion was as ludicrous as the Great Wall of China itself and proved just as useless, though both were erected at great expense.

Over the years the situation has improved. Analysts do declare prominently on their research notes when they work for the *house stockbroker*, that is the broker retained to act for the company. Some brokers will issue research on companies where they are house broker but avoid making recommendations.

You should certainly err on the side of scepticism when reading research. In the case of house brokers you should consider whether recommendations ought to be downgraded one or two levels, assuming that 'buy' should really read 'hold' and 'hold' should read 'sell'. I cannot remember ever seeing a sell recommendation from a house broker.

Analysts at different stockbrokers can and do take different views of the same company. No-one, not even the experts, gets it right all the time. Usually it is a difference between 'buy' from one analyst and 'hold' from another or 'hold' and 'sell' but occasionally one analyst sees the stock as a buy and another advises selling. The following table summarises some brokers' recommendations on Barclays shares over a two-month period in 2007.

Table 9: sample brokers' recommendations for Barclays shares

Date	Broker	Recommendation	Change
10 Aug 07	Panmure Gordon	Sell	DownGrade
02 Aug 07	Panmure Gordon	Hold	Reiteration
02 Aug 07	Cazenove	Outperform	Reiteration
23 Jul 07	Evolution Securities	Reduce	Reiteration
13 Jul 07	HSBC	Neutral	Upgrade
06 Jun 07	JP Morgan	Neutral	Reiteration

You may have noticed these occasional discrepancies in one of the Saturday or Sunday newspapers that summarise brokers' tips.

You must, as always, use your own judgement. Try to assess whose arguments seem more convincing. Keep a note of these clashes and check later how the shares of the company in question fared. You may get a feel for which stockbroker tends to get it right more often.

Analysts tend to make far more buy recommendations than sell, as the former tends to generate more orders. Also they don't win business from a company by telling investors to sell its shares!

Newspapers and magazines

The financial pages of the newspapers are excellent ways to keep in touch with events on the stock market and the economy in general. You probably buy a newspaper anyway so the City pages come free.

Do try taking different papers, both on weekdays and on Sunday, to get a feel for which provides the level of City coverage that suits you.

Not all provide share tips. Among the dailies, Tempus in *The Times*, Questor in *The Daily Telegraph* and The Investment Column in *The Independent* offer share tips. For the Sundays, only Midas in the *Mail on Sunday* and Share Tips in *The Sunday Telegraph* tip individual shares.

There are two weekly magazines with tips columns. *The Investors Chronicle*, published on Fridays, offers Mr Bearbull, while *Shares* magazine comes out on Thursdays and carries Plays of the Week. Both these magazines may carry tips in other sections.

The two magazines and some weekend newspapers also carry summaries of tips from stockbrokers.

Unlike analysts, financial journalists are unlikely to have passed any examination for registration with the Financial Services Authority, nor will the newspapers they write for be supervised by the FSA.

The Financial Services Act 1996 specifically absolved newspapers from the regulatory regime unless they were *tip sheets* – that is, they specifically existed to tip shares. We have seen since then the gradual disappearance or scaling back of share tipping from some publications to avoid attracting the attentions of the FSA.

Newspapers therefore do not have to comply with stricter rules on matters such as avoiding a conflict of interest; any rules that are followed are voluntary ones set by the newspaper. This is unlikely to go beyond expecting any journalist writing on a company to declare to the City Editor any shareholding he or she has in that company.

Nonetheless, tip columns are edited by, and largely written by, financial journalists specialising in this field. I have written for three of the publications listed above and can vouch for the general integrity of their tips columns (though I will leave the readers to decide on their general success).

As with the analysts working for stockbrokers, you can find conflicting advice in newspaper tips columns. Once again, investors must use their own judgement to decide which arguments seem more convincing and which tipsters tend to get it right most of the time. Newspaper tipsters mercifully tend to be clearer and simpler in their categories of advice. You will mainly find 'buy', 'hold' and 'sell' but you will also come across 'avoid' and 'take profits'.

This last category is often qualified with the advice to sell half your shares and keep the other half. The reasoning is that if the shares fall back after a good run you have at least banked some profits at the top of the market. If the shares continue to rise, then you are still getting some benefit from the ones you hung onto.

One drawback with newspaper tips is that there is a fixed space available each day so set number of companies will be covered irrespective of whether news and events justify the selection.

Also, share prices for companies tipped in the papers can move substantially so you may not be able to trade at the recommended price. This is particularly important if you ask your stockbroker to buy at best price – you may find yourself paying rather more than you intended, as traders have got in before you and bid the price up.

20.

Jargon Busting

Every way of life has its own language and the stock market is no exception. I have tried in this book to keep explanations as simple as possible but there are some often used expressions that are worth learning about.

In particular, you will see name tags attached to shares:

- *Blue chips*
  The largest companies on the stock market. The term is often used about any company in the FTSE 100.

- *Recovery stocks*
  Shares that have taken a battering but could be turning the corner, perhaps because of new management or improving markets.

- *Cyclical stocks*
  Companies that see their fortunes rise and fall with cycles in the economy. As the economy slows, theirs are the products that consumers can most easily manage without. Examples would be furniture retailers and leisure groups. Transport groups could suffer as fewer goods are moved and fewer people travel to work

- *Counter-cyclical stocks*
  These companies do well out of a recession but are abandoned in the good times. A budget clothing retailer would expect to sell more when people are out of work but most of us prefer something stylish to wear when we go out to celebrate a pay rise.

- *Defensive stocks*
  These companies expect their share price to hold up well when shares prices are falling. Supermarkets should survive a downturn because we still have to eat.

- *Growth stocks*
  Small companies that are growing strongly and are expected to continue to do so.

- *Value stocks*
  Companies whose shares are cheap given their excellent prospects.

- *Penny stocks*
  Shares that have fallen below 10p on the stock market.

- *Shells*
  Companies that have cash but do not have any operating companies.

Those pesky animals

Bulls and bears

Most people have heard of bulls and bears, the most popular exhibits in the stock market zoo:

- **Bulls** are the optimists, the ones who buy shares in the touching belief that the good times will roll for ever and a day. If you think shares will go up, you are a bull.

- **Bears** are the gloomy pessimists, the Victor Meldrews who see the end of the world rapidly approaching. If you think shares will go down, you are a bear.

You can mix and match your animal instincts. You may be bearish about the market as a whole but bullish about an individual company or vice versa.

Stags

While bulls and bears abound freely, *stags* have been almost hunted to extinction. A stag buys newly issued shares with the intention of selling for a quick profit. They were a protected species under Margaret Thatcher, who fed them on a rich diet of privatisation issues.

The theory is that when a company is floated on the stock market it will be priced just below its real value. This (it is hoped by the financial advisers) avoids the ignominy of new issues dropping heavily as soon as they are released. As the shares gently rise in value, the advisers bathe in the healthy glow of a successful flotation and a large fee.

Stags attempt to spot when the advisers under-price the share issue. They apply for shares then sell in the market at a substantially higher price.

Alas, most new share issues are placed with institutional investors because that is cheaper than offering them all round. So the opportunities for stagging are few and far between for private investors.

Dead cat bounce

Better to be a stag than a cat, the unfortunate creature that features in the *dead cat bounce*. Squeamish readers and cat lovers should look away now.

If you go to the top of a tall building and drop a dead cat over the edge it will bounce, though not very high. Please do not try this at home and rest assured that the author has never conducted such an experiment with any creature, dead or alive.

When shares have fallen heavily, they often reach a point where they bounce up a little. This may be because shareholders who sold out at the top decide it is time to get back in or because new investors judge that the fall has gone far enough.

Alas, in dire circumstances the shares may well start falling again after a short pause. That short-lived minor recovery is known as a dead cat bounce.

Case study: Bloomsbury Publishing

Figure 5: share price of Bloomsbury Publishing

Harry Potter worked a fair amount of magic for shareholders in Bloomsbury Publishing for the best part of a decade but the dangers of being too heavily dependent on a single product became evident in late 2006, a year in which JK Rowling's creation donned his invisibility cloak and no book appeared. Bloomsbury issued a profit warning after the stock market closed on December 11th, citing lower than expected pre-Christmas sales, and its shares fell off a Quidditch stick, dropping from 310p to 220p.

We then saw a classic dead cat bounce as the shares struggled back up to 256p on December 29th. No doubt those who had done very well holding Bloomsbury shares but who had taken profits were tempted back in at the sharply lower levels, especially as the seventh Potter tome was surely on its way.

Not even Potter could bring this cat back to life, though, and the shares subsided in a gentler but more persistent fall back below the 220p floor. Word on February 1st 2007 that the final year of Harry Potter's schooldays, 'Deathly Hallows', would appear the following July brought only the tiniest of flickers to the dead cat's tail as Bloomsbury admitted that it remained cautious in the light of challenging market conditions.

Catching falling knives

A short walk from the menagerie to the kitchen takes us to the concept of catching falling knives. Sometimes the shares really do recovery. It isn't a dead cat bounce after all.

Now the name of the game is to buy while shares are cheap and sell when they are dear. If you can catch a share after it has fallen heavily and hold it as it recovers you make a nice profit.

This is, however, a dangerous game, rather like trying to catch knives dropping from the top of the same building as the dead cat.

You might grab the handle, in other words catch a share that has been oversold and will recovery as soon as the panic is over.

On the other hand, you could grab the blade. You now own shares that keep falling. Snatching at falling shares is a dangerous business. They could be falling for a very good reason – the company could even be going bust.

21.

Mergers And Acquisitions

Takeovers are arguably the most exciting aspect of stock market investing because it is one way that investors can make substantial profits in a short space of time. Newspapers love takeovers because they often involve companies with colourful personalities as chief executive; so there is generally plenty of press coverage, which means shareholders can easily keep themselves aware of any developments.

It is quite likely that at some stage you will invest in a company that is subsequently involved in a takeover or a merger (a merger is when two companies join together to become one). This activity is referred to as *mergers and acquisitions*, more often than not abbreviated to *M&A*.

Takeovers may be:

* *Friendly*: a friendly bid is where the two sides agree on a price and the target company recommends its shareholders to accept.

* *Hostile*: in a hostile bid, the target company tries to fight off the bidder and advises its shareholders to reject the offer.

Takeovers and share prices

In takeovers, the share price of the target company tends to rise, sometimes even before the bid is announced. This may happen because news of an approach leaks out or because investors sense that a particular company is susceptible to an offer. Since investors privy to inside information can make large profits from buying shares before a bid is announced, the procedure is governed by a strict *Takeover Code*. Bidders believe that takeovers create the opportunity to increase sales or cut costs, which is why they are usually willing to pay a *bid premium,* that is they offer more than the prevailing market price. The share price of a bidding company often falls as its shareholders fret over whether it is paying too high a premium.

Although takeovers can happen at any time, they are understandably more prevalent when shares are comparatively cheap. A surge of takeover activity can be a sign that the stock market is rising again after a fall; similarly the sudden drying up of takeovers can signal that the stock market has peaked.

Example: Japan Tobacco takeover of Gallaher Group

On 6 Dec 2006 the shares of Gallaher Group, one of the UK's biggest cigarette manufacturers, closed at 979p. After the market closed that day, Gallaher announced that it had received "an approach from an unnamed party". It went on to say that the approach was, "preliminary and there can be no assurance that an offer will be made." The following day, 7 December, it was revealed that Japan Tobacco was launching a takeover bid for Gallaher, whose shares consequently soared that day and closed at 1190p.

Japan Tobacco later confirmed it was making a bid at 1140p a share – an offer that was subsequently accepted by Gallaher's shareholders.

Chart 8: Japan Tobacco's takeover of Gallaher Group

Looking at the chart above of Gallaher over the bid period a couple of observations can be made:

1. Although official news of a takeover was not released by Gallaher until 6 December 2006, the shares started climbing strongly from a month or so previously – suggesting that someone knew of the impending bid.

2. After Japan Tobacco announced its bid price of 1140p per share (and the takeover was uncontested), the shares quickly settled into a small trading range around the bid price until the takeover was complete.

Do takeovers work?

Opinions vary on whether takeovers really work. Among the most spectacular successes was Hanson, built into an transatlantic conglomerate giant in the 1980s by an astute strategy of buying undervalued companies.

On the other hand, some boards seem merely to want to flex their muscles in a show of strength or they have run out of ideas for growing the businesses they already have. Often takeovers end up destroying rather than creating value, although that is all too often forgotten when the next wave of takeovers comes along.

One group of people always gain in a takeover situation, whatever the outcome. An army of highly paid advisers drawn from each company's lawyers, stockbrokers, financial advisers and PR experts pore over all the details at great and expensive length.

Takeovers

In a takeover, one company buys another. We shall refer to the company making the bid as the *bidder* and the company on the receiving end as the *target company*. The bidder is also referred to as the *offeror* and, less formally in the press, as a *predator* or a *suitor*.

The majority of takeovers and mergers involve companies in the same line of business. This is known as a *trade deal*. These deals are popular because there are advantages in putting two companies with complementary businesses together.

It may be possible to grow the combined businesses by selling goods and services to each other's customers or by creating a nationwide business instead of two regional ones. Working together to boost sales is known as *synergy*.

There could also be cost savings, for example from combining the sales staffs or from putting manufacturing facilities under one roof. This is *cost cutting* – although companies will often refer to it as synergy because this sounds better than saying staff will be fired to save money.

If the bid is from a company outside the sector it is referred to as a *financial bid*. In this case there are no synergies to be achieved as the businesses cannot be combined, although it may be possible to boost sales through more dynamic management. The bidder will probably be hoping to make the operations more profitable by cutting costs.

Takeover Panel

Where one company buys, or attempts to buy, another company, the procedure is governed by a strict set of rules called the *Takeover Code* and is supervised by the *Takeover Panel*.

Takeover rules have been tightened considerably over the years for the good of all investors.

The Takeover Panel has 34 members, including representatives of professional bodies such as the Association of British Insurers, the British Bankers' Association, the Confederation of British Industry and the Institute of Chartered Accountants in England and Wales.

This is not a cosy Old Boys' club, nor is it a protection racket to preserve the rights of City bigwigs. It has developed a justified reputation for fairness and even handedness. It does not flinch from bringing large quoted companies and their City advisers to book in order to ensure fairness for all, including small shareholders. The Takeover Panel expects the spirit of the Code to be followed as well as the letter of the law.

When, in March 2007, Marks & Spencer chief executive Stuart Rose remarked at a conference that supermarket chain J Sainsbury looked 'interesting', M&S called a hasty meeting of directors and rushed out a statement saying that they had dropped any ideas of launching a bid for Sainsbury. They knew that if they did not bite the bullet immediately, the Takeover Panel would be on to them next morning demanding an explanation for what might seem a fairly innocuous remark.

The Takeover Code has been developed since 1968, not only to promote fairness but also to ensure that takeovers and takeover battles are conducted in an orderly fashion. Its rules apply even before a bid is formally launched and it governs not only the companies involved in the bid but all their advisers.

The code does not rule on whether a takeover is set at a fair price or makes commercial sense. That is a matter for the shareholders to decide.

You can read the full details of the extensive and thorough code by logging on to the Takeover Panel's website (www.thetakeoverpanel.org.uk). In the next two chapters we shall pick out the main points that affect small shareholders.

Mergers

In a merger, two companies agree to come together to form a new group. A new company will be set up and shareholders in both existing companies will receive new shares in the new group in place of their existing holdings.

The size of the allocations will depend on the sizes of the respective companies that are merging. Assuming that both companies are quoted on the stock exchange, the ratio will be broadly in line with their market capitalisations.

Case study: ITV

One of the most high profile mergers in the UK in recent years was between media groups Granada and Carlton Communications. The two companies had gradually bought up most of the ITV franchises between them and the next logical step was for Granada, based in Manchester and traditionally strong in the North of England, and London-based Carlton to come together to form one nationwide ITV company to meet the growing competition from satellite and digital broadcasters.

The merger was agreed in October 2002 but was delayed by an investigation by the Competition Commission (a government body appointed to curb the creation of monopolies). The merger was allowed to go ahead late in 2003 and was completed in February 2004.

Because Granada was roughly twice as large as Carlton, about two thirds of the new ITV was divided among Granada shareholders while Carlton shareholders received the other third.

Granada shareholders were given one new ITV share for every Granada share held, while Carlton shareholders received 1.9386 ITV shares for each Carlton share held. This rather precise conversion rate was calculated to give a fair division of ownership in the new company.

The higher conversion rate for Carlton was because there were about four times as many Granada shares in issue as Carlton ones.

Michael Green, chairman of Carlton, became chairman of the merged group while Granada's executive chairman Charles Allen became chief executive of ITV. Three non-executive directors from each company joined the merged board.

22.

Before A Bid

A bid can be brewing for many months before it is formally announced. Sometimes talks are held and the bidder walks away only to return with new proposals when it feels that the target company will be more receptive.

These informal talks, out of the glare of publicity, can be very useful in determining whether it is worth pursuing a potential bid or in negotiating terms acceptable to all parties.

Time was when companies refused to comment on market rumours but nowadays the Takeover Panel requires them to issue statements when the market gets wind of a potential bid, which is quite often.

When companies must issue a statement

Although it is not necessary to comment on a rumour that is utterly without foundation, target companies must own up if a firm offer has been received, or there is *untoward movement* in the share price after an undisclosed approach has been received or when negotiations are taking place.

There is no specific ruling about how untoward a movement in the share price has to be. It used to be 10% but a more flexible approach is taken these days and companies tend to err on the side of revealing all when their shares move sharply upwards.

A company cannot be wrong in making an announcement but it can regret keeping quiet and subsequently having to admit it has been hiding an approach. If in doubt, companies can consult the Takeover Panel, which leans on the side of making an announcement if it is in the interests of shareholders.

The bidder must put any proposal to the board of the target company before it makes it a public pronouncement. That is not only courtesy, it gives the target company's directors chance to assess the proposal and decide on what stance to take.

Getting the two sides together at an early stage, before any announcement is made, can be advantageous to shareholders. It means that the share price of the target company is not distorted by the announcement of an approach that has no chance of success. On the other hand, it gives the target company the opportunity to try to persuade the bidder to offer a higher price.

At this stage there is no obligation on either side to make a public announcement. It is impossible to say how many approaches are never revealed but it is likely that they are heavily in the majority.

When news of a takeover bid leaks out

Inevitably, though, word of an approach sometimes leaks out. It shouldn't, and it is against the Code, but it happens. The manifestation of the leak comes in a sharp rise in the shares of the target company. When that happens, the target company is obliged to reveal the approach.

This is usually done by issuing an anodyne and fairly vague statement along the lines that an approach has been received that may or may not lead to an offer; the approach is very preliminary and there is no guarantee that a bid will be made.

Occasionally matters are at a more advanced stage. The target company may be able to say that it is in discussions with the potential bidder and possibly indicate a proposed price per share.

An approach can be tentative or an outright threat or anywhere in between.

At the most tentative level, a predator and target company will simply be having *preliminary talks* with no proposal of any kind on the table.

Pre-conditional offer

The next level up is a *pre-conditional offer*. The predator has put forward a proposal in principle but there are conditions to be met before this is turned into a firm offer. These conditions usually include the right to look at the target company's accounts in confidence, referred to as carrying out *due diligence*, and it may still be necessary for the predator to raise enough finance to pay for the bid. Pre-conditional offers are often rejected out of hand by the target company as being too vague.

Indicative bid

Somewhere in the middle of the scale in an *indicative bid*. The predator indicates the price it intends to offer for the target company's shares.

Indicative bids may be rejected by the directors of the target company. You will often see phrases such as 'seriously undervalues the company and its prospects'. It is the duty of the target company's board, in the interests of their shareholders, to try to drive the bid price as high as possible.

Indicative bids are frequently dismissed as *opportunistic*, a pretty meaningless term, since every bid is made because someone sees an opportunity.

Firm offer

At the top end of the scale is a *firm offer*. The predator has finance available and has put forward a bid price. This has to be taken seriously by the target company although the offer can still be rejected as too low.

These announcements would normally come from the target company but the predator may sometimes make an announcement even if no bid is yet on the table. This could be to state an intention to make a bid if finance can be raised, or it could be a decision not to bid after all.

If a predator rules out making a bid it cannot then make an offer for at least six months except in special circumstances. The main exceptions are if another predator makes an offer or if the target company agrees to submit to a firm bid.

Offer period

A company may be deemed to be in an *offer period* even before a formal proposal is put forward, provided a serious possibility of a bid has arisen.

During an offer period all shareholders holding more than 1% of the shares in the target company must announce any share purchases or sales they make. Directors in the target company are barred from dealing in the shares.

The company is also obliged to make far more disclosures of all its activities, day-to-day matters than it would normally not have to tell the stock exchange about. This is to ensure nothing affecting the bid is hidden.

Takeovers are time consuming for the company secretary, who has the unenviable task of issuing all the information. They are expensive for the target company, which will be paying advisers to assist in evaluating any bid.

Put up or shut up

When one or more bidders have indicated that they might make an offer for a target company but are dithering, the Takeover Panel may set a deadline by which a decision on whether to bid or not must be taken. This is known as a *put up or shut up* ruling.

The aim is to avoid having a potential target company being distracted from its day-to-day business by having the threat of a takeover hanging over it indefinitely.

Mandatory offers

One key rule of the Takeover Code is that if a major shareholder buys more shares and its stake rises above 30% it is obliged to make a bid for all the rest of the shares. The aim is to spare minority shareholders from getting locked into a company where a large shareholder has gained control.

A mandate is a command. Do not be confused by the way that politicians misuse the word to mean permission. A mandatory offer is one that *must* be made.

The bid must be at least equal to the highest price that the bidder has paid for shares during the previous 12 months.

You may wonder why 30%. After all, you need just over 50% to gain full control of a company. With more than half the shares you can then outvote all the rest of the shareholders put together.

However, it is possible for a large shareholder to gain effective control of a company with less than 50%. If one shareholder has 45% of a company and the rest of the shares are divided among a large number of holdings, it is highly unlikely that the small shareholders would be able to band together as an opposing force.

In any company there are always shareholders who fail to vote at all while many more slavishly back the existing board.

Stock exchanges in various parts of the world have considered at what level a major shareholder is likely to take effective control. Any figure is inevitably arbitrary but it is there to protect small shareholders.

The Australian Stock Exchange settled on 20% as the threshold. That does seem, though, to be rather on the low side. London chose 30% as a fair compromise.

Substantial acquisition rules

Potential predators are restricted in the number of shares they can buy before they launch a full bid.

This may seem a bit unfair on the predator but the rule protects shareholders in the target company who might otherwise sell in the market at a lower price without realising something is afoot.

The rule also restricts predators that are seeking to build a sizeable stake without making a bid.

It is perfectly permissible for a predator to buy one large stake of any size in the target company, bearing in mind that going above 30% automatically sparks a mandatory offer to all shareholders at the same price or better. A large shareholder seeking to get out may be only too happy to part with a slab of shares at one go. Dribbling a large holding out into the market drives the price progressively lower.

Predators buying from more than one source cannot buy a total of more than 10% of the target company within a seven day period if that takes them above 15%. This rule is waived if the predator announces an intention to make a bid.

If the share buying takes the predator above 30%, then a bid is mandatory anyway.

Inducement and break fees

A target company may pay some or all of the predator's costs in launching a bid. This may seem rather outrageous, like a little fish paying the whale for the privilege of being eaten alive, but it does have its uses and can work very well for the shareholders in the target company.

A potential predator may be reluctant to embark on an offer without a reasonable assurance of success. Bids can be expensive, with advisers to be paid and a whole barrowload of paperwork to be sent out to all the target company's shareholders.

An *inducement fee* is paid to get the predator to conduct due diligence and, assuming nothing nasty has emerged, to table a formal offer. This fee is payable if the target company's shareholders reject the offer. It may even be payable if the predator decides not to make a bid.

The aim is to provoke interest in the hope that other potential bidders will emerge once they know that the target company is *in play*.

Break fees are more common. They recompense the bidding company in the case of an agreed bid if the target company's board withdraws its recommendation or a third party steps in with a better offer and wins.

The Takeover Code sets a limit to the size of break fees, so if you are a shareholder in a target company you can rest assured that your cash is not being dished out wantonly.

As with inducement fees, break fees can provoke an offer when otherwise none would be forthcoming. As long as you end up with a better offer for your shares than you could have got by selling on the stock market, why worry?

Due diligence

Bidders naturally want to be quite sure the target company is in good health and they will ask to be allowed to carry out due diligence.

Assuming that the proposed takeover is a friendly one, this is no problem and the target company will allow the bidder to take a detailed look at its accounts (also called looking at the *books*).

The general financial health of the target company will be pretty well known because it can be gleaned from the twice-yearly results statements the company is required to release.

However, companies hold back data that they consider to be commercially sensitive, information that they think would help the rivals they are competing against in the marketplace.

Accountants, legal experts and other consultants for the predator will sign undertakings not to divulge any secrets before being allowed to look at information such as the terms of bank loans, contracts with customers, tenancy agreements, employment contracts and other minutiae that could have an impact on the value of the business.

The process can be expensive if those highly paid consultants are poring over the books for several weeks. They will be looking for ways to boost sales or, more likely, to save money by cutting out duplicated costs.

Due diligence is a bit tricky when the bid is hostile, since the target company will be reluctant to allow an unfriendly bidder to see its innermost secrets, especially if the approach has come from a rival.

This issue arose when supermarket group William Morrison first attempted to take over rival Safeway in 2004.

Tesco, Asda and Sainsbury all expressed an interest in bidding for Safeway but were refused access to the books because Safeway reasonably suspected that the other supermarket groups were merely attempting to derail the Morrison bid rather than trying to put together a genuine alternative offer.

The Takeover Code says that all genuine potential bidders must be treated equally, whether the approach is friendly or hostile, so any information given to one suitor must be made available to all. Safeway would have been obliged to treat all potential bidders equally but as it happened the Morrison bid was the subject of a competition inquiry and it subsequently became clear that its rivals would not be permitted to bid for Safeway.

23.

A Bid Is Launched

A takeover bid is generally good news if you hold shares in the target company but is usually not particularly welcome for shareholders in the predator company.

That is because takeovers are normally pitched at a higher level than the stock market price of the target company. This is known as the *bid premium*.

The following table shows a selection of bids that were made in the second quarter of 2007. The market price is the stock market price of the shares on the day before the approach was revealed.

Table 10: sample takeover bids

Target	Sector	Bidder	Market price	Bid price	Premium
EMI	Music	Terra Firma	222p	265p	19.4%
Dobbies	Garden centres	Tesco	1,217p	1,500p	23.2%
Oasis Healthcare	Dentists	Duke St.	47p	82p	74.4%
Sanctuary	Music	Vivendi	11.25p	20p	77.8%

Bidders prefer to get the backing of the target company's board. If they do, then it is an *agreed* or *recommended bid*.

An agreed bid has a greater chance of success, since the target company's board is urging its own shareholders to accept. The offer has to be sufficiently generous to win this recommendation.

If the target company rejects the approach, the bidder may still go ahead and launch a *hostile bid*. The terms still have to be attractive enough to tempt the target company's shareholders to accept. After all, you could sell on the stock market if you wanted to get out.

Hence shares in the target company will usually go up when a bid is announced.

Just occasionally a bid may be pitched below the stock market price. This can happen when a company finds itself in dire financial trouble and a rescuer emerges, but only at a lower price than the stock market was hoping for.

Irrevocable acceptances

In an agreed bid, the directors of the target company will be accepting the offer for any shares that they own and it is possible that other large shareholders will agree to accept also.

It is quite usual in these circumstances for such acceptances to be binding. The backing of a sizeable number of shares, possibly even a majority of them, may be a crucial factor in persuading a predator to launch a bid.

The directors, and any other shareholders who have been privy to the negotiations, may make an irrevocable promise to accept the bid even if a better offer comes along. Alternatively, they may reserve the right to switch sides if a higher offer is made.

Hostile bids

A bid can still be made even if it is rejected by the board of the target company. A spurned suitor can appeal directly to the target company's shareholders who, after all, own the company. This is known as *going hostile*.

A hostile bidder is entitled to obtain a copy of the target company's share register and to communicate with all the people who are on it.

The bidder will send documents setting out its arguments for taking over the company and urging the shareholders to accept. The target company will also write to its shareholders setting out the reasons for rejecting the offer.

If you own shares in a company that is the subject of a takeover offer it is in your interests to read these documents and to weigh up the arguments before deciding whether to accept or reject the offer.

The offeror

Now let us consider bids from the point of view of investors in the offeror. Benefits are distinctly less obvious. Indeed, a bidding company may see its share price fall as investors worry about whether it is overpaying for the proposed acquisition.

Assuming that the bid succeeds, there will be immediate costs to pay over and above the price of buying the target company. If cash has been borrowed from the bank to fund the bid, then the interest bill will go up. Redundancies to remove duplication in the workforce will have to be paid for.

Management time will have to be spent in integrating the target company into its new owner and there may be additional costs in making the computer systems compatible or meshing the distribution networks.

The benefits, in contrast, take time to come through.

The bidding company will say when it announces its bid whether it expects the acquisition to be *earnings neutral* in the first year, that is when earnings per share for the group would be roughly the same with or without the acquisition.

If the bidder has struck a good bargain, the acquisition could be *earnings enhancing* from the start, in other words any costs will be immediately more than offset by the gains.

More likely than not, it will take some months, possibly even a couple of years, before the acquisition starts to show its full potential, in which case the takeover will initially be *earnings dilutive*, that is earnings per share will be reduced at first before rising in subsequent years.

Bid terms

Any company making a firm bid must state the price per share that it is offering and must be certain that it has sufficient financial backing if it is offering cash.

The bidder can offer cash, some of its own shares or a combination of both in return for the target company's shares. It must clearly state its terms.

Here is an example of each type of bid taken from the first half of 2007–

- *All cash*: Austrian brickmaker Wienerberger bid 247p a share for UK rival Baggeridge Brick.

- *All shares*: Investec, a specialist banking group, offered 0.7 of one of its own shares for each share in Kensington, a provider of mortgages for people who have difficult in obtaining loans from banks or building societies.

- *Cash and shares*: Thompson, the Canadian financial news and data provider, offered 352.5p plus 0.16 of its own shares for each share in Reuters, its UK based rival.

Individual shareholders in the target company are not obliged to accept an offer even if it is recommended by the company's own board. As we shall see later in this section when we discuss the bid timetable, it can be good tactics to hold off for a while. Do not be bullied into taking the offer immediately by the tone of the offer document that is sent out to the target company's shareholders.

Bids may be subject to conditions set by the bidder. If the acquisition is a large one, the bidder may need to seek the permission of its own shareholders to proceed. Where the takeover is between two similar companies it is usual for the bid to be conditional on not being referred to the Competition Commission or the European Commission, either of whom could block it as being against the public interest.

The bid will certainly be conditional on a minimum number of acceptances. This will normally be set at 50% plus one share, which gives a majority stake, but it can be higher, even as high as 90%.

Bidders often stipulate 90% acceptances as a condition when they launch the bid but reduce the level to 50% subsequently. They always have the right to *waive*, that is to drop, conditions but not to introduce new ones.

If and when all the conditions have been met or have been waived by the bidder, the bid will be declared *unconditional*, which means the takeover has succeeded.

Compulsory share purchases

Where a company makes a bid and gains acceptances for at least 90% of the target company's shares it is entitled to force the tiny remaining minority to accept the bid.

The bidder normally wants full control of the target company and having a few errant shareholders left in is a real nuisance. Separate accounts have to be drawn up for the target company and sent to the remaining shareholders.

At the same time, it is really not in your interests to be trapped into a company with just a handful of other tiny investors. You will be at the mercy of a massive shareholder who doesn't want you hanging around and you will not be able to sell your shares because they will have been delisted from the stock exchange.

On the other hand, if a sizeable minority of shareholders refuse to accept, it may be because the bid price was too low and in that case they are entitled to hang on and hope that they will be offered more at some time in the future.

So again, the 90% threshold may be an arbitrary figure but it is a reasonable level and it is there to balance the interests of all parties.

Loan notes

Most bids come with a *loan note alternative*, that is, you can accept loan notes rather than cash to the value of your shareholdings.

A loan note is an IOU. You are letting the successful bidder hang on to the cash it owes you rather than taking the money for your shares immediately.

The reason for this alternative is that accepting a bid will usually create a capital gain and investors who have used up their capital gains allowance for the year will face a tax liability.

There is no capital gain on the loan note until you cash it in, so you can spread your gain over more than one tax year.

A set rate of interest will be paid on the loan notes, usually payable every six months. The issuer of the notes will let you cash them in on certain specified dates each year.

Reverse takeovers

In most takeovers a large company takes over a smaller one. This is because the smaller company comes at a lower price and the larger company will either have enough cash to pay outright or it will be able to issue new shares without swamping its own existing shareholders.

There are, however, occasions when a smaller company makes a bid for a larger one. Frozen food retailer Iceland got to the prominence it enjoys today by snapping up the much larger but somewhat complacent Bejam chain.

The outcome of a *reverse takeover* may not be straightforward. If the takeover is paid for in shares in the bidding company rather than cash then the shareholders in the target company may actually end up with more than half the shares in the enlarged group.

The most common reason for a reverse takeover is a technical device to give a large unquoted company a stock market listing. So instead of the big company buying the little one and losing the listing, the quoted company bids for the larger unquoted company, paying in its own quoted shares rather than in cash. In such cases management of the larger company usually takes charge of the enlarged group.

Scheme of arrangement

Instead of making a normal takeover offer, a predator may attempt to take control of a target company through what is known as a *scheme of arrangement*.

The biggest advantage for the bidder is that it is simpler and cheaper than an ordinary takeover. For one thing, it does not attract stamp duty and it can be a considerably faster process than a formal takeover.

Under a bid, the predator is setting out to buy the shares of each shareholder individually. With a scheme of arrangement, the bidder is asking for permission to buy the entire company at one fell swoop.

For the scheme to be approved shareholders in the target company must vote for it and where 50% of the shares must be voted and 75% of the votes cast must be in favour. Shares already owned by the bidding company are not counted.

A 51% acceptance is not good enough, as it is with an ordinary bid. The 75% rule is to protect the rights of small shareholders in the target company so they are not steamrollered into accepting.

Success means that any dissenters are overridden automatically and they must take the offer. It is not necessary to gain the support of 90% of the target company in order to force out the minority.

One disadvantage for the predator is that a scheme of arrangement is more vulnerable to a competing offer from another bidder. There is no point in the predator buying shares in the target company because these cannot be counted in the vote, so it is possible for a rival to buy enough shares in the target company on the stock market to block the arrangement.

A scheme of arrangement requires the support and cooperation of the board of the target company. This is because it is the target company, not the bidder, that actually puts the arrangements in place by calling an extraordinary general meeting of all its shareholders. It is also why this arrangement is often used when two companies are merging rather than one taking over the other.

Since the target company is supporting the offer, it is usual for the 75% hurdle to be cleared but that does not always happen if a concerted campaign can be waged against the deal.

Partial offers and tender offers

It is possible for a predator to ask the Takeover Panel for permission to make a *partial bid* in which it will end up with a sizeable stake but less than 100% of the target company, and possibly less than the 30% level at which control is deemed to have been secured.

Case study: Countrywide

The estate agent received an offer worth 569p a share from some of its own executives, backed by investment group 3i, in December 2006.

The independent directors in Countrywide, the ones who would not be staying on to run the company, decided to support the offer, arguing that no alternative bid had been received, nor was there any indication that any other party was even considering one. The terms were above the existing stock market share price.

However, larger shareholders opposed the bid on the grounds that it undervalued the company and at the EGM to consider the scheme of arrangement in January 2007 the voting was 57.8% in favour and 42.2% against.

The scheme of arrangement needed the backing of 75% of votes cast. Although the antis were in the minority, this was a notably large rejection vote.

On 22 February, 2007, American investment group Apollo Management indicated it was planning to offer 590p a share provided it could attract support from large shareholders in Countrywide.

Having satisfied itself that it would avoid the ignominy suffered by the proposed management buyout, Apollo duly launched its bid in March 2007. Once again, a scheme of arrangement was used, this time successfully.

The partial offer can be in cash or in the bidder's own shares.

At least 50% of shareholders not connected with the bidder need to give their approval for a partial bid to go ahead.

These safeguards are to protect ordinary shareholders, who are at risk of getting locked into a company that has effectively been taken over without the bidder paying a premium for the privilege.

There are other restrictions. For instance, partial offers where the suitor ends up with more than 30% of the shares – the level at which it would normally be required to make a full bid – will not normally get the go-ahead from the Panel if the bidder has bought shares in the target company during the previous 12 months.

Also, if the predator intends to end up with between 30% and 50% of the target company it must declare the precise number of shares it intends to buy and it cannot declare the partial offer unconditional unless it secures that amount.

Shareholders should be wary of the possibility that the predator will make a full bid some time in the near future. If a full bid is made at a higher price than the partial offer, the shareholders who accepted the partial offer miss out on the difference.

The bidder may state that it does not intend to make a full bid. In that case it cannot bid for at least six months. Nor can it buy any more shares in the market for 12 months if the partial offer is successful.

Tender offers are cash only and the bidder must not end up with more than 30% of the target company.

The offer may be at a price fixed by the bidder. If the offer is *oversubscribed*, that is acceptances for more than the required number of shares are received, the acceptances are scaled down. For example, if a tender offer was made for 10% of a target company and shareholders accepted for 20% of the shares, each accepting shareholder would keep half their shares and sell the other half to the bidder.

The alternative is for the bidder to set the maximum price it is prepared to pay and for accepting shareholders to state the minimum price they are prepared to accept at or below that level.

If the tender offer is not fully taken up, then all accepting shareholders will get the maximum price stipulated by the bidder. If the offer is oversubscribed, then the *strike price* is set at the lowest level that fills the tender. All shareholders accepting at or below the strike price will receive the strike price for all the shares they tendered.

Bidders can stipulate a minimum acceptance level for the tender, so if very few shareholders accept the offer can be dropped. The minimum level is, though, quite low, usually 1% of the target company and in any case no more than 5%. This is to prevent a potential bidder from testing how the land lies without making a serious commitment.

Stub equity

On rare occasions shareholders in a target company may be offered the opportunity of taking cash for most of their holdings while retaining a small stake in either the bidder or the target company, remaining as minority shareholders.

They are left with the 'stub' of their holdings, hence the name *stub equity*. The theory is that these shareholders get the best of both worlds. They receive a nice dollop of cash for most of their holdings but they still get some benefit if the target company does really well under its new owners.

The big advantage for the bidder is that less cash has to be found to fund the bid, since it is not buying all the shares.

Stub equity fell into disrepute donkey's years ago when a supermarket chain called Gateway (later resurrected as Somerfield) was the subject of a bid battle. A private equity firm by the fanciful name of Isosceles won by grossly overpaying. To cut the cost of its pyrrhic victory as best it could, Isosceles offered stub equity in the now debt-laden group.

The stub fell in value to the point where you couldn't give it away and nothing more was heard on the subject in this country for about 20 years when the notion was dragged up again in the takeover of property company Canary Wharf.

Offering stub equity may prove to be a sop to critics who argue that predators, particularly private equity companies, generate huge returns by taking companies private, loading them up with debt so they get their cash back, then refloating them on the stock market.

However, that raises the conclusion that they have underpaid in the first place. Shareholders accepting stub equity are locked in as minority shareholders in a company that is taken private so it may be very difficult to get the rest of their investment out until the company is refloated, possibly several years down the line.

Competition regulators

However much you may welcome a takeover bid as an investor, there are regulators in the UK, Europe, the US and elsewhere who see things from a different angle. Their job is to ensure that putting two companies together does not leave too much power concentrated in too few hands.

In the UK, the Office of Fair Trading screens mergers and takeovers. Most are waved through but if the OFT has doubts it will refer the case to the Competition Commission for a more thorough investigation.

The Competition Commission used to be called the Monopolies Commission until jokes about 'why is there only one Monopolies Commission?' led to a name change.

The OFT referral will be based on whether a deal poses the threat of a substantial lessening of competition. There is no specific level, but if the two merging companies have more than 25% of a particular market between them the deal is likely to be referred.

The OFT may not be looking at the whole market. For example, when cruise lines Carnival and Royal Caribbean were fighting a bid battle for

UK rival P&O Princess, the OFT did not consider the whole holidays market but simply whether either bidder would end up with a stranglehold on the cruise market.

The OFT may also consider whether a company will gain a monopoly within a particular region or even smaller area. For instance, it wants to see more than one supermarket and more than one betting shop in each town.

Competition Commission reports normally take up to six months to investigate, although this can be extended. The Commission reports its findings to the Secretary of State for Trade and Industry.

The minister must approve a merger or takeover if the Competition Commission rules that it should be allowed. However, the minister has a choice whether or not to accept a ruling against a merger or takeover.

Regulators in Europe and the US have the power to block a deal. While they will leave any purely UK combination of businesses to the OFT, they may intervene if international markets are affected.

24.

Bid Timetable

The Takeover Code sets out a timetable designed to create an orderly procedure and to allow all parties adequate opportunity to safeguard their positions without letting the proceedings drag out for an undue length of time.

The offer document spelling out all the relevant details must be posted to the target company's shareholders within 28 days of the announcement of a definite offer. Initially the offer will then be open for at least 21 days to allow time for shareholders in the target company to accept if they wish to do so.

The target company's board is obliged to write to its own shareholders setting out its opinion of the merits of the bid and is expected to advise acceptance or rejection of the bid, giving its reasons.

The bidder can allow the bid to lapse at the first closing date. In other words it can scrap the bid and walk away after the 21 days are up. Alternatively, the bidder can extend the acceptance period but if the bid is not wholly unconditional 60 days after the offer document was sent out then the bid has failed.

If a rival bid is made part way through the bid timetable, the timetable will start again.

Where a bid fails, the bidder cannot launch a new bid for at least 12 months except under certain conditions. These are if the directors of the target company recommend a new offer or if another firm bidder emerges for the target company.

Takeover timetable

Day	Event
Day 0	The day that the bidder posts documents to shareholders in the target company.
Day 14	The last day on which the target company's board can advise shareholders whether to accept the bid. If the advice is to reject the bid, then the document setting out the reasons, known as the defence document, must be issued by this date.
Day 21	An offer must remain open for acceptances for at least 21 days to give shareholders in the target company reasonable time to make up their minds. This is the first closing date and the bidder can drop the offer at this point, declare the bid unconditional if it already has enough acceptances, or extend it for two weeks.
Day 35	If the offer was declared unconditional as to acceptances on Day 21 then the offer can be closed at this point as the waverers have now had ample time to accept.
Day 39	If the bid is hostile and it has not yet gone unconditional, this is the last date on which the target company can issue further information bolstering its defence.
Day 42	Any shareholder who has already accepted an offer can withdraw that acceptance after this point. The idea is to allow shareholders the opportunity to switch sides if a better offer comes along.
Day 46	The last date on which the bidder can raise its offer. Shareholders in the target company now have 14 days in which to take a final decision on whether to accept.
Day 60	It's D-Day. Either the bidder has enough acceptances to declare the bid unconditional as to acceptances or that's the end of the story for another 12 months. No more extensions are allowed.
Day 81	Any other outstanding conditions must be fulfilled or waived by this day so the offer can go fully unconditional.
Day 95	The bidder must pay up within 14 days of the offer going fully unconditional so this is the last day to settle up.

25.

Bid Battles

Competing bidders

If you are really lucky, two or more bidders will compete to buy your company. In this case the bidding will escalate as each bid tops the previous one.

Example: Reg Vardy

The battle of the car dealers, with Pendragon and Lookers pitched against each other in a fight to take over Reg Vardy, provides several important lessons that are well worth looking at in a little detail.

Note that all the bids were recommended by the Vardy board. Do not be too hard on the directors for recommending that shareholders should accept the lower bids. Sometimes it is good to get one bid on the table by recommending it so that other bidders know the target company is in play, in other words it is willing to consider bid offers.

Overleaf is a timetable of what happened:

Date	Event
Late October, 2005	Reg Vardy shares move above 600p and continue rising.
Nov 15, 2005	Reg Vardy shares close at 662p
Nov 16, 2005	Vardy reveals an unsolicited approach from Pendragon indicating offer at 750p a share. Vardy shares briefly top 750p but settle slightly lower.
Nov 29, 2005	Vardy says it has received two other approaches at higher than 750p. Talks with all prospective bidders continue. Vardy shares rise to 790p.
Dec 5, 2005	Pendragon offers 800p cash, Vardy directors advise shareholders to accept. Some shareholders, including Vardy directors and Vardy family, pledge to accept for holdings totalling 27% of Vardy. First closing date 28 December. Vardy shares remain above 800p.
Dec 12, 2005	Lookers says it is considering rival bid, making good progress on raising finance. Vardy shares trade at 820-830p
Dec 29, 2005	Pendragon claims acceptances for 28.3%, extends offer to January 18, 2006; Vardy shares remain around 825p.
Jan 17, 2006	Lookers bids 875p. Vardy board switches recommendation to accept Lookers bid. Vardy shares jump to 910p.
Jan 19, 2006	Pendragon has acceptances for 28.4% at second closing date, extends offer to 1 February, urges Vardy shareholders to accept.
Jan 27, 2006	Pendragon proposes three-way merger of Pendragon, Lookers and Vardy. Lookers rejects proposal. Vardy shares fall to 855p.
Feb 3, 2006	Takeover Panel gives Pendragon until March 10 to announce firm bid for Lookers or drop the idea. Pendragon buys 6.3m Reg Vardy shares at 900p each and raises bid for Vardy to 900p. Vardy shares rise to 895p.
Feb 6, 2006	Vardy board drops support for Lookers bid, switches back to recommending Pendragon's increase offer. Vardy shares rise briefly just above 900p.
Feb 7, 2006	Lookers drops offer for Vardy.
Feb 8, 2006	Pendragon takes its stake in Vardy to 40.4%. Vardy shares now stay just below 900p offer price.
Feb 14, 2006	Pendragon has acceptances for 55% of Vardy, declares the bid unconditional.

Commentary on the Vardy bid

First of all, Reg Vardy shares started moving a good two weeks before any announcement was made. It looks as if someone got wind of a possible bid!

Chart 9: Reg Vardy, example of a bid battle

When Pendragon did make its move, the shares initially settled just below the suggested offer price. This is a normal reaction. If investors are confident that a firm offer will be forthcoming the gap below the proposed price will be quite small; if the bid is more doubtful then the gap will be larger.

The *discount* between the stock market price and the proposed offer price took into account various factors.

Firstly, you could sell Vardy shares in the market immediately for 745p and get your cash now rather than wait for the bid to go through. Sure, you could get an extra 5p by holding on but that was the price of not having the use of your cash immediately. Think of it as an interest payment covering the time difference.

Secondly, the discount allowed for the possibility that the bid might fail. Pendragon could change its mind or a majority of Vardy shareholders might refuse to accept. When a bid fails you expect the target company's shares to drop back to the level they were trading at before the approach.

In this case there was every reason to believe that Pendragon would bid. Where a potential bidder indicates a price it is clear that the approach is serious. The size of the gap between the stock market price and the indicative offer reflects the City's view of the balance between the risk of the bid being dropped and the reward if it succeeds.

All that changed two weeks later when Reg Vardy revealed that it had received two other approaches. The potential reward – that someone else would bid more – now had to be weighed against the possible, and now highly unlikely, risk of no bid at all.

Where there is a potential bid battle it is almost always worth hanging on to see if the rivals try to outbid each other but investors had the choice, if they felt nervous, of taking a very nice profit while the opportunity was there.

Pendragon came in with what it hoped was a *knock-out bid* of 800p a share. The possibility of a rival proposal persuaded it to offer 50p a share more than it intended but it hoped that 800p was high enough to deter any other suitors.

No such luck. Lookers started to go round the financial institutions raising the cash for a higher bid. The Takeover Code stipulates that a bidder must have enough cash in place to fund an offer before it is made.

Vardy shareholders were now feeling more confident. They believed that with a definite bid on the table the worst that would happen was that they would get 800p a share. So the shares traded at a higher level, factoring in the potential reward of a higher bid.

Pendragon failed to get more than 50% of the shares when the first deadline for acceptances arrives. At this point Pendragon could, had it wished to do so, have allowed the bid to lapse. However, it kept its options open by keeping the bid open and setting a second deadline.

Note that a handful of Vardy shareholders accepted the Pendragon offer despite the fact that they could have got a higher price by selling their shares on the stock market. Some small shareholders seem to think that any document that says 'sign me' has to be signed. They need to read this book.

In due course Lookers came up with a higher offer. This then became the *floor* for the Vardy share price as the balance of risk and reward shifted upwards.

Pendragon attempted to muddy the waters by proposing that all three car dealers get together but was given a *put up or shut up* ultimatum by the Takeover Panel. Make a bid for Lookers by a date set by the Panel or drop the idea. This type of ultimatum is issued when the Panel feels that shareholders are unable to make an informed judgement because the position is unclear.

The Panel's decision was justified by the fall in Reg Vardy's share price. The confusion over whether Pendragon would try to thwart Lookers by buying Lookers as well as Vardy was unsettling investors by making it difficult for them to make an informed decision.

The 'put up or shut up' ruling did the trick. Pendragon bought a large slab of Reg Vardy shares for 900p. Under the Takeover Code, Pendragon was obliged to offer the same terms to all shareholders. That meant one large shareholder was not allowed to strike a special deal while small shareholders received less favourable treatment. Takeovers have to be as fair as possible to all.

Although Vardy shares briefly edged above the 900p level of the revised bid on hopes that Lookers would still offer more, the chances had now swung heavily in favour of assuming that this was as good as it was going to get.

The two main reasons were that Lookers was unlikely to bid any higher – remember that 900p was already 150p more than Pendragon had originally hoped to pay and 100p more than the first bid that the Vardy board had recommended – and that Pendragon was building up a large stake by buying Vardy shares so it was well on the way to gaining 50%.

When Lookers dropped out, Pendragon was able to raise its holding in Vardy to 40% very quickly.

Once acceptances topped 50% Pendragon had control of Vardy and it declared its bid unconditional. In other words, all conditions set by Pendragon in launching the bid had been met and the bid had succeeded.

Accelerated bids

Where there is a bid auction and the rivals keep making progressively higher bids there is a danger of the process dragging on for an inordinately long time, since the bid timetable goes back to Day 0 every time a new offer document is posted.

To speed up the process, the Takeover Panel may hold an accelerated auction in which the rivals put forward competing bids over several days rather than weeks until one bidder outbids the rest. This would probably have happened in the case of Reg Vardy had proceedings dragged on any longer.

26.

Management Buyouts

Instead of a takeover by an external company, companies may be bought by a team of managers who take the company private. In other words, the company continues as a separate entity but it withdraws its stock market quotation.

The offer to buy all the shares may come from the exiting executives of the target company. This is known as a *management buyout* (MBO) because the existing management is buying out all the other shareholders. The logic behind this type of deal is that no-one should understand a company better than its managers – if they think the company is undervalued in the market they might be tempted to launch an MBO.

Sometimes the offer comes from a set of managers who are unconnected to the company and who think they can run it better than the existing executives. This is known as a *management buy-in*.

Very rarely, the proposed new team comprises some existing and some new executives – which a City wag dubbed as a *bimbo* (or *buy in/management buy out*).

All these situations are nowadays generally referred to as *MBOs* and we shall use this term irrespective of where the new bosses are coming from.

The management will almost certainly be getting financial backing from another source unless one of them is very rich. Banks may provide a loan or, more likely, venture capitalists are providing the cash.

Venture capitalists are groups of wealthy individuals who – among other activities – specialise in buying companies that they feel are undervalued by the stock market, so the immediate suspicion with any MBO is that someone is trying to get your company on the cheap.

Case study: Alliance Boots

Alliance Boots was formed in mid-2006 by the merger of Alliance Unichem and Boots, two well known chains of chemists' shops. Eight months later, on 9 March 2007, Alliance Boots revealed that it had received an approach that might lead to a bid for the company.

Chart 10: Alliance Boots, example of a management buyout

Alliance Boots shares had suddenly moved up from 822p to 855p just before 2.30pm that afternoon, a gain of 4%. To its credit, the company had a statement out through the stock exchange in three-quarters of an hour.

The approach, it turned out, had come from the executive deputy chairman, Stefano Pessina, backed by private equity, and he was considering an offer of £10 a share.

The fact that the deputy chairman was plotting a coup when he was there to look after the business on behalf of all shareholders raised questions over a possible conflict of interest. Pessina had previously controlled the Alliance Unichem side of the business before the merger and suspicions were inevitably raised that he helped to engineer the merger so that he could gain control of a business twice the size.

He had an unfair advantage over any other possible bidders in deciding what to offer because he was more familiar with the company, its trading and its finances.

Furthermore, he personally owned 15% of the shares, making it easier for him to reach 51% and harder for a rival to do so.

Given that he apparently wanted to keep most of the executives in place after taking over the company, one wondered why he believed Alliance Boots would make more money as a private concern than as a public listed company.

On the positive side, Pessina and his backers were prepared to pay well over the prevailing stock market share price in what looked quite a generous proposal and any other potential bidders had the opportunity to come back with a higher offer if they so wished.

Last but not least, shareholders in Alliance Boots suddenly had the opportunity to sell their shares on the stock market for an extra 175p. They also had the option of hanging on in the hopes of a higher bid with little fear that the shares would fall back.

The rest of the board met to consider the approach in the absence of Pessina and the marketing director, who also came from Alliance Unichem and was supporting Pessina's plans.

The independent directors argued that it was too soon after the merger to be thinking of more changes and they rejected the proposal as undervaluing the company.

Pessina subsequently offered 1040p a share, then 1090p and finally 1139p as first the independent directors, then rival bid interest, forced him higher.

Existing management should know the company inside out and if they see hidden value there, shareholders are entitled to wonder why that value has not been unlocked for the benefit of all shareholders already.

Those directors who are not going to be involved in the company after it has been taken private are referred to as *independent directors*. They will usually be the non-executives. There role will be to represent the existing shareholders in the target company and not to side with any executives involved in the offer.

Since the independent directors have nothing to gain from the MBO – indeed, they will be losing their directorships and the fees they are paid – they can attempt to extract as high a bid as possible on behalf of the ordinary shareholders.

Some independent directors are rather better at this than others and there have been occasions where they have dug their heels in and refused to recommend acceptance of an MBO.

On other occasions they may lack a little spine in standing up to the executives. They have, after all, sat round the same boardroom table month after month and may have too cosy a relationship to start fighting.

In these circumstances your fate is often in their hands.

One factor that may help is that if the managers try to get ownership of the company on the cheap it is possible that another bidder will step forward and offer more. Don't count on it, but it does happen.

Another possibility is that major shareholders may revolt. We noted in the previous chapter that this is what happened at Countrywide, the estate agents chain, where management attempted to buy the company with financial backing from investment group 3i. This buyout was actually recommended by the independent directors but ran into strong opposition and was voted down by shareholders at an EGM.

MBOs often emerge when the company is doing badly. Although one can wonder how a management team that has failed to deliver value for shareholders can sort the company out after taking it private.

APPENDIX

Useful Websites

Organisations

Association of Investment Companies – www.theaic.co.uk

Association of Private Client Investment Managers and Stockbrokers – www.apcims.co.uk

Financial Services Authority – www.fsa.gov.uk

London Stock Exchange – www.londonstockexchange.com

Takeover Panel – www.thetakeoverpanel.org.uk

Free and subscription sites

BBC – www.bbc.co.uk

Citywire – www.citywire.co.uk

Hemscott – www.hemscott.co.uk

InvestEgate – www.investegate.co.uk

Motley Fool – www.fool.co.uk

Reuters – www.reuters.co.uk

Sharescope – www.sharescope.co.uk

Index

C